LIFE THROUGH LOSS

Facing Your Pain
Finding Your Purpose

GAIL PORTER

To Heidi ~
I pray this book
will encourage you
in your own
life journey.
Gail

Cover design by Terri Oesterreich

Cover photo by Jeff Leimbach jlphoto-graphic.com

Published by EA Books, Inc.
EABooksOnLine.com

"I've known Gail for more than forty years and have seen her growing passion to minister through writing, speaking and coaching. Because of her experience in touching the heart needs of others and because of her own pain of extensive loss in her family, Gail is uniquely equipped to write this book, *Life through Loss*."

STEVE DOUGLASS, president, Campus Crusade for Christ International/Cru

"Gail Porter is a radiant example of the love of Christ. Her countenance revealed the sincerity of her faith as she has lived through very difficult circumstances."

VONETTE BRIGHT, author, speaker, co-founder of Campus Crusade for Christ International/Cru

"When I started reading *Life through Loss* I couldn't put it down. Having lost my son and my brother, I lived Gail's emotions and felt her pain. She honestly shares strengths and weaknesses of family members when telling her story. It is refreshing and encouraging to see how her interaction with remaining family members enhanced their relationships after each loss. Gail's vulnerability, faith, and willingness to let God use her loss to change her life are evident throughout the pages of her book."

SUSAN GIARRUSSO, wife, mother, marketing director

"Gail Porter gently guides you into the emotional storm of anticipatory grief and encourages the sorrowful to recognize the almighty presence of God that uplifts the brokenhearted."

JUDY VOSS, Registered Nurse, Certified Hospice and Palliative Care Nurse, author of *Finding Joy in Sorrow* and *Compassion and Joy*

"Because of her hands-on experience with deep losses, Gail Porter can compassionately and tenderly minister to those who grieve. As a physician, and because of my own experience of losing my mother and my only sister, I have personally seen death and dying. Gail's God-breathed stories in *Life through Loss*, offer hope, joy, peace, and purpose to those who face life-threatening illnesses with their loved ones."

ANGELITA N. KURLE, M.D.

"I have known and worked with Gail for many years, and she is an amazing woman of God and genuine friend. She brings us into her personal world as she grapples with what she calls her "cascading loss" of family members. We can grieve our own journeys of loss alongside her, and then she lifts us up so we can hope again. She reveals how we take the next steps in discovering the special purposes God has for us in our undesired, unexpected seasons of life."

JUDY DOUGLASS, writer, speaker, encourager,
Campus Crusade for Christ International/Cru

Books Co-Authored By Gail Porter

THE SIGNIFICANT WOMAN
Connecting with God, Discovering Your Personal Mission

SOARING
Going from where you are to where you want to be

www.TheSignificantWoman.com

DEDICATION

In memory of my sister Addi
who showed me how to participate in life

"Everything fits into a pattern for good,

to those who love Me and are called

according to My design and purpose."

Romans 8:28
(The Amplified Bible)

CONTENTS

INTRODUCTION

Loss invades our lives without permission. It arrives unsolicited and unwelcomed, bringing with it pain, devastation, and despair. When loved ones die, those left behind often ask, "How will I survive without them?" "How will I face each new day?"

I am one of those left behind. Illness and death cascaded into my life, leaving insufficient time to grieve before saying goodbye to yet another loved one. Most of their journeys began and ended with cancer.

While caregiving and encouraging family members, I observed how they faced unwanted and unexpected pain with God's help. In His tender and intimate way, God prepared them to live in their heavenly home.

Walking these individual journeys with them opened my eyes to see that my past relationships with my family followed an intentional plan of detachment. I'd never invited them to become a part of my personal life. My aloofness protected me from their life situations that could upset my predictable world.

My assignment at Campus Crusade for Christ's Asian headquarters in the Philippines lasted twenty-three years. Naturally, being a world away from them prevented me from daily involvement in their lives. The distance also fueled my silent plan.

After returning to the United States, phone calls and

occasional visits provided an opportunity to learn about family happenings while still guarding my personal space. I remained detached until disaster struck.

One after another, family members became ill and faced uncertain futures. Their desperate needs began to overpower my inner resistance. Although fear of inadequacy and risk of rejection surfaced, I couldn't deny the looming crises. Relinquishing my safe place as a spectator, I finally stepped forward.

My involvement ushered me into the hearts of those who were suffering. It also thrust me into the lives of their adult children. Surprisingly, the new closeness felt natural, rewarding.

My decision to walk on God's path of heart commitment to my family unleashed His power in me. He equipped me to help meet overwhelming needs as I watched each loved one draw nearer to heaven. As they finished God's ordained journey and left this earth, I expected my world to shrink. Instead, it expanded. A single, independent woman all my life, I now cared deeply about younger family members who had captured my heart.

Raw grief and razor-sharp pain engulfed all of us as each loved one departed. Slowly our mutual losses melted the distance between us. Life and death issues cropped up in our conversations. Sharing heartaches, fears, and disappointments opened windows to one another's struggles and dilemmas. Healing took place between family members. Relationships blossomed.

God wove cords of connection between us where none existed before. Recognizing His work in our lives softened my sadness and served as a reminder of His faithfulness during devastating times.

Through loss God exposed my emotional detachment, broke down my walls of aloofness, and overpowered my fears. He showed me how to build deep relationships and become the kind of person He wanted me to be all along. All of this took place according to God's carefully-crafted plan: "Everything fits into a pattern for good, to those who love Me and are called according to My design and purpose" Romans 8:28 (The Amplified Bible).

Perhaps you have experienced loss and pain in your life, or you are facing impending loss. I pray that in the midst of your pain you will notice new facets of God's heart and His love for you.

My desire is that these stories will inspire you, instill courage to move through your pain, and restore your emotional strength to fight discouragement and despair so you can hope again. If you look for the connections God is weaving in your life and the lives of others, your discoveries can create a desire to move forward in spite of your feelings. God longs for you to discover His purpose and plan for your new season of life.

God says in Deuteronomy 30:19, "…I have set before you life and death, the blessing and the curse. So choose life in order that you may live, you and your descendants."

PART 1

CASCADING LOSSES

LEFT BEHIND

I stood at Mom's bedside, listening to the whoosh of the respirator and staring at the tangled tubes framing her sweet but silent face. Hope died. The doctor's quiet pronouncement—"irreversible coma and irreversible brain damage"—screamed motherless to me. She was heaven bound, but I would soon be left behind.

Sadness, grief, and loneliness engulfed me. The pain of impending separation carved a deep ravine in my heart. Longings haunted me: *When do I get to go to Heaven? When will I be able to experience heavenly joy? Why not now?*

In my younger days those kinds of questions never entered my mind. During my third year of college, my maternal grandfather died from congestive heart failure at seventy-eight. More than twenty years later, my grandmother—whom we affectionately called Grandmartie—died of natural causes five months short of 100.

Their deaths surfaced memories we'd built together. I remembered the time Granddaddy took me on two outings in one day. At the dairy farm he tested me on the names of the cows. I smiled with pleasure when I scored high on his pop quiz.

Our next stop took us to the zoo. Hand in hand we greeted a variety of God's creatures. Fortunately, Granddaddy had lifted me into his arms before we reached the lion's cage. The deafening roar from the lion's wide, twisted mouth terrified me. Bursting into tears, I buried my head in my grandfather's coat. With his strong arms wrapped around me, I felt safe again.

On school days, before my mother and father arrived from work, I scuttled to my grandmother's home a few blocks away. Warmth and a sense of belonging surrounded me the moment I opened her door and bounded up the back stairs. Grandmartie's happy hum filled my ears before I entered her sunny kitchen.

"Hi, honey. Ready for some eggnog?" she'd often ask.

Nodding, I'd climb onto a chair in their cozy breakfast nook, waiting to slurp my treat.

She'd always say yes when I asked, "Grandmartie, may I look in your attic today?"

Each discovery thrilled me: her old dolls, colorful dresses from earlier days, a soft hairpiece crafted from a large swatch of her beautiful, brown hair.

Many afternoons I cuddled next to her while she read to me, her soft arm around my shoulder. She assumed each voice in the story. My favorite dialogs were ones that captured her natural Southern accent.

From an early age she taught me about God's love. Speaking often of Jesus as her friend, she recounted many ways He had helped her in difficult situations. Her life and words became her legacy to me, the foundation for a deep love of God.

Granddaddy and Grandmartie filled the role of family patriarch and matriarch. In later years my brother and I resisted their strictness, yet we never forgot their unconditional love for us.

When they passed away, I missed them but their deaths were not devastating to me. They had lived full lives. Their time to rest in heaven had arrived. Though they remained a cherished part of my life, I let go and moved on.

But the untimely critical condition of my seventy-four-year-old mother stunned me. She had often joked with family and friends, "I'm preparing to live to at least ninety. Just look at Mother!"

One morning, before heading out the door to go to work at Campus Crusade's Asian Headquarters in Baguio, Philippines, the phone rang. My roommate Ella answered it.

She turned to me. "It's your uncle."

My mind whirled as my uncle's words came across the line, "Gail, I called to tell you your mother fell down the back stairs of her house and fractured her skull. You need to come home."

Ella offered to accompany me to Manila. She captured two seats on the small commuter flight leaving that morning from our mountain town. Our travel agent booked a seat out of Manila to the United States the following day.

In the evening I called Aunt Elia for a progress report. Mom remained on a respirator.

After tossing and turning all night in my hotel bed, I said to Ella, "What if Mom doesn't survive?"

"She will," Ella said.

I clung to that hope as I sat rigid and wide awake on the long flight home.

Aunt Elia and Uncle Miles met me at the Portland airport. When I caught sight of Aunt Elia's face and looked into her eyes, I knew the situation must have changed since our last conversation. We drove the short distance to the hospital, trying to think of things to say. Uncle Miles remained in the waiting room. As Aunt Elia and I walked down the long, silent hallway I reached for her hand.

My heart cried, *how will I survive without Mom?* In the face of inevitable loss I realized how much I still needed her companionship and love. My independent spirit, my failure to share my heart with her, and my pattern of simply assuming her life was moving along smoothly, had robbed me of many hours with this wonderful woman I called Mom.

Now I would never hear her voice again. Never be able to ask for her wise advice. Never have a chance to assure her how much I loved and admired her.

She had worked more than thirty years for a well-known insurance company. Coworkers—men and women from their twenties to their sixties—enjoyed her company. She gained a reputation as an excellent problem solver, always rising to the challenge.

At age sixty her company sent her back to school to take computer classes in preparation for a new responsibility. In town on vacation, I drove her to the university. This time the roles were reversed—the daughter watched her mother walk with a youthful stride toward her college class.

After retirement she looked forward to many activities,

including her weekly date with longtime friend Dorothy. They took turns meeting at each other's homes for a lunch visit and working on their latest handicraft item.

One time Dorothy's roommate Elaine came along. Elaine cleaned up the lunch dishes and sat down in the living room to enjoy her book. Years later Elaine recounted what happened next.

"I began to hear laughter from the den where they were working," she told me. "Their giggles turned into roars of laugher. I walked down the hallway and slowly opened the door.

"'What's going on?' I asked. They both burst out laughing again.

"After further conversation I solved the mystery. They were working in a small, closed room and the odor from the glue gun made them high!"

"That's so funny," I said as I laughed with Elaine, "especially coming from those two reserved women who would have never dared do such a thing."

Looking back on my growing-up years, I marveled at Mom's ability to work full time, keep up the garden, maintain an organized home, do the laundry, prepare nourishing meals and school lunches, and assist my brother and me with homework.

Each year she baked and invited all of their friends to an annual Christmas Open House. She fed her passion for homemaking and entertaining while silently bearing the burden of an unhappy marriage.

Their difference in personality, values, and life perspective

11

caused constant underlying tension between my parents. They divorced when I was thirteen and my brother Greig fourteen.

The familiar family structure remained intact, with my grandparents as the pivotal people. Dad's parents had died before my birth. I knew no uncles on my dad's side since he and his two brothers no longer communicated.

After the divorce Dad and I saw each other occasionally. I didn't yearn for more.

Meanwhile, Mom guided me in her quiet way and listened to my endless chatter about nothing. When I became a young adult she told me, "I'll give you any advice you ask for."

One of the first decisions I discussed with her related to my desire to join the staff of Campus Crusade following my college graduation.

"I'm glad about the work you've chosen. Do you really think you might be assigned to California? That'd be nice."

After six years in California my boss and his wife transitioned to another Christian organization. I looked for other opportunities within Campus Crusade. Nothing enticed me. Then one day our personnel director called me into her office.

"Gail, would you be willing to live in Seoul, Korea, for six months and help prepare for the international delegates who will attend our training conference there?"

Her invitation surprised me. I'd never thought about an overseas assignment. Strangely, my heart embraced this opportunity without fear.

"Yes!" I blurted out.

"Well, pray about the opportunity this weekend and let me know on Monday," she said.

I felt confident my answer represented God's desire, but wondered what Mom would think. Early Saturday morning I crawled out of my cozy bed, and tiptoed down the wooden stairs of my apartment while my roommates slept.

With each step my mind played out a probable outcome. *She's used to my play-it-safe lifestyle. This kind of news from her only daughter will shock her. She'll probably give in to her own fears and try to convince me not to fly off into the unknown.*

Pulling the phone from the kitchen ledge to the dining room table, I slid into the nearest chair. My fingers shook as I dialed Mom's number.

"Hello?"

"Hi Mom. Thought I'd give you a call," I began.

"Oh, good to hear from you. How was your week?"

"Well, pretty good, but something a little unusual happened," I explained. "You know I've asked about a different assignment with Campus Crusade."

"Yes. Has something interesting come up?" she said.

"Well, our personnel director asked if I'd be willing to live in Korea for six months to help with an international conference."

I waited. Silence.

Suddenly she said, "Well, maybe I could visit you there."

What happened to her typical fears? Her unexpected enthusiasm

13

gave me the freedom to embrace my next step of faith.

Moment of Surrender

Memories flowed freely as I stood at my Mom's hospital bed that night. Seeing her lying there in a coma, unable to communicate, brought a deepening sense of aloneness, as if the sun were setting permanently. She'd lighted my way from childhood to adulthood. Her guidance flowed without conditions, and she relished the time we spent together without demanding it. Her willing sacrifices provided greater opportunities for me. No one could ever take her place.

I didn't want to say goodbye, but I sensed God prompting me to let go. Mom had opened her heart to Jesus at the age of twelve so I knew I would talk with her again, just not here. Through my tears, I surrendered her to Him, trying to picture the welcome she'd receive in heaven.

As we left mother's hospital room, Aunt Elia said, "Your brother chose not to come now, but he's waiting for your call."

As soon as we reached my aunt's home, I dialed Greig's number. The moment I heard his voice, I blurted out, "Greig, when I saw Mom I sensed she was already in heaven."

"I believe she's in heaven."

His confident response intrigued me. As far as I knew, he still refused to let God enter his life. Yet, we both clung to the hope of seeing our mother again in heaven.

Because of the doctor's declaration of irreversible coma and irreversible brain damage, our family faced a traumatic decision. We couldn't avoid Mom's frequent reminder, "I never want to live if I'm surviving only on a respirator. Let me go."

We knew only the respirator was keeping her alive. We asked the doctor's advice. He said, "We suggest that families turn the respirator lower, because it often allows the patient to simply slip away." We gave our permission, and agonized throughout the next two days while she remained in a coma.

We longed for Mom to wake up, with her energy and enthusiasm restored, yet we realized that would never happen. The doctor reconfirmed that her brain was no longer functioning. As a family, we knew the time had come to turn off the respirator. We alerted the hospital of our decision.

As Aunt Elia and I prepared to go sit with her at the hospital, the phone rang.

"Hello?"

Silently Aunt Elia handed me the phone.

The nurse gently informed me Mom had passed away. My heart sank. We were too late. She was gone.

In that dreaded moment I expected emptiness and sadness to overtake me. Instead, joy rose in my heart. *I finally feel close to you again, Mom.*

Aunt Elia cried while I hugged her. Hearing her sobs, my uncle rushed in from the porch and received the news all of us anticipated but none of us wanted to hear.

"Do you mind if I play some praise songs?" I asked.

"Of course not," Aunt Elia replied quietly.

Playing the piano always ushered me into God's presence. That's where I longed to be at that moment.

The next morning after a shower, I padded back to the extra bedroom in my aunt's home. Sadness flooded my heart as reality settled in. How am I going to survive without Mom? I whispered.

The answer came as though Mom stood at my side. *You'll be all right, honey.*

Hope rose in my heart. Mother lived in heaven and I still lived here—but she knew I would be all right. In that moment, sorrow loosened its grip.

Celebrating Life

Working with the pastor at my mother's church, my aunt and I planned the memorial service. No one in the family felt emotionally equipped to share from the platform, so we contributed stories for him to weave into his message.

Greig and his sons Jake and Casey flew out from South Carolina. In spite of the occasion, we cherished the relaxed, personal time together. We stayed in our mother's home without her.

The day of the memorial service dawned. Greig and I were grateful we could share this experience together. We joined the rest of the family where beautiful flower arrangements graced the front of the church. The organist played some of mother's favorite hymns.

The pastor talked about Mom's family, church and community involvement, her work and some of her hobbies. When he mentioned knitting, Casey glanced up at me with a big smile. I knew he remembered watching his grandmother knit during her visits.

The choir director stood up to sing mother's requested song, "I Believe." His deep, melodious voice lifted our spirits. As he sat down I thought, *seems like there're more verses to that song.*

Later he explained, "Halfway through the song I suddenly realized I'd lost a friend I enjoyed and admired. I couldn't continue singing."

One of mother's friends told me after the service, "I brought my handkerchief because I expected the service to be very sad. But I didn't cry because you helped us focus on the wonderful person your mother was."

During the reception that followed the service, Greig greeted mother's friends in a gracious and friendly way. Normally reserved in a crowd, his engagement symbolized his desire to honor her. Many people hadn't seen him since he moved away at twenty-one, so together we recalled funny stories and good memories.

A few days later, the family gathered around the pool at my aunt's home. None of us could ignore Mom's absence. She loved to swim there. Though sad, that day became an important time of building new memories that would carry us through the sorrowful days ahead.

Walking Forward

The hole in my heart seemed bottomless. An email from my

friend Sandy in Manila comforted me.

"Gail, I want you to know I am committed to praying for you every day for two years while you grieve the loss of your mother. A widow friend of mine once told me, 'I have learned that every loss leaves a space only God's presence can fill.'"

During the next few weeks at my aunt and uncle's home, we shared memories and laughed and cried together. New warmth filled my heart when their son Cary told me, "Gail, now you are the daughter our mother never had."

The day came to return to the Philippines. After loving hugs from my aunt and uncle, I shuffled to the plane. Yearning for God's comfort, I opened my Bible to Isaiah 61:1-3. "The Spirit of the Sovereign Lord is upon me, for the Lord has…sent me to comfort the brokenhearted…. To all who mourn in Israel, he will give a crown of beauty for ashes, a joyous blessing instead of mourning, festive praise instead of despair. In their righteousness, they will be like great oaks that the Lord has planted for his own glory."

I wanted to become like one of those oaks God has planted for His glory. Through my righteousness, which would flow from trusting Him daily and allowing Him to control my life, I could bring Him glory. He would rebuild me, bringing about His plan for my future. Peace draped itself around my heart like a soft blanket.

A period of mourning lay ahead. Yet God promised to give me a crown of beauty, joyous blessing, and festive praise. Some days I experienced deep sadness, triggered by unexpected memories. Other days I smiled at pictures of my mother, thankful to God for giving her to me.

My friend Susan, who had lost her son, gave me *Grieving the Loss of Those You Love*. I clung to words in that small book. They brought new perspective to the pain I felt.

"Regardless of the way you feel right now, it can be helpful to know it's possible for all this pain to be redeemed by God, to know he can turn this pain into something useful, something from which you can learn—if not today, then sometime in the future. When we realize that this pain—this life—is but a single moment in the scope of eternity… [it becomes] a life-saving truth…. We can truthfully and joyfully shout that this pain is insignificant in light of the fact we 'are being transformed into his likeness with every-increasing glory which comes from the Lord, who is the Spirit' (2 Corinthians 3:18)."

In the midst of my pain, I began to notice a transformation. In the past, my need for acceptance prevented me from letting my friends catch a glimpse of the real me. Gradually I sensed a desire to come out of hiding. I asked God to give me courage to share with others about my pain, hurt, disappointments, problems, and weaknesses.

My new openness led to more authentic relationships with family and colleagues. In the last ten years of ministry in the Philippines, I experienced greater fulfillment than I had during all the previous years combined.

END OF AN ERA

Having Dad in my life eased the sadness of losing Mom. He and I had come a long way in building a meaningful relationship and he showed his love and support in many ways.

Dad had met Connie at work several years after my parents divorced. A tall, beautiful, and humorous woman, Connie attracted Dad's attention. They fell in love and married during my first year in college.

After their marriage, I didn't feel the need to stay in touch with Dad as much. I lived 80 miles away on my college campus. One Sunday they initiated a visit. I welcomed them, showed them around my sorority and the campus, and enjoyed lunch together. Then I refocused on my studies.

As graduation approached, my mentor suggested I visit them and explain my plan to work in California. I knew contacting them was right in God's eyes.

"Hi, Dad," I said when he answered the phone. "Wondering if maybe I could visit you and Connie?" My trembling voice threatened to reveal my false confidence.

Immediately he replied, "Of course. When can you come?"

I pulled up in their driveway on the designated day. With my heart beating and my mind questioning how this visit would go, I climbed the front stairs of their small yellow house.

"We're so glad to see you," they said as they opened the screen door and embraced me. Their strong hugs and welcoming words alleviated my fears.

Halfway through our conversation, I took a deep breath and said, "I wanted to tell you I've decided to work with a Christian organization called Campus Crusade for Christ after I graduate. My first assignment will be in California."

"Sounds good," Dad said. Connie agreed.

Their positive response to my decision bridged the gap in our relationship. I appreciated the way Connie told me more about her life that day. Her husband had died at thirty-eight, leaving her with two young children. Now her grown son Bernie lived in Montana. Her daughter Addi lived nearby. I'd met Addi at the wedding, but looked forward to getting to know her as my new stepsister.

Through the years I discovered how similar Dad and Connie were in every area of life. They built a wonderful relationship of unconditional love and affection that continued throughout their twenty-nine years of marriage. I loved seeing Dad happy and felt grateful that Connie had become my stepmother.

Connie told me they laughed together about something every day. "In the mornings I'm usually in the kitchen in my robe fixing the coffee when Charlie wanders out of the bedroom. He'll always say, 'Hi beautiful!' I tell him, 'Charlie, you need glasses.'"

Dad grew up being called Chuck. Connie called him Charlie. That endearing name fit him perfectly.

Addi liked to describe them as "umbilical twins." They were

together twenty-four hours a day and relished every minute. Frequently they went dancing after their night shift. Both tall and stately, they made a handsome couple on the dance floor.

"You should see them when we go out," Addi told me. "Gradually everyone on the floor moves away so they can watch them dance."

Connie took care to make me feel special. During one weekend visit, she took my measurements when I arrived and sewed a beige velour top for me by the time I left.

Mr. Fix-It

When Dad had married into the family, Connie and Addi quickly discerned one of his most helpful skills. He could fix anything.

One day, Addi's young son David had asked to go to his Grandpa's house. As Addi parked in the driveway, David bounced out of the car.

Climbing up the back stairs as fast as his chubby little legs could carry him, he cried out, "Grandpa, my tricycle won't work!"

"Well, bring it on in. Let's see what the problem might be."

After depositing David's red tricycle in Dad's tool shed, Addi sought out one of the twin recliners in the spacious double wide mobile home. She nestled in for a catch-up time with her mother, sipping a cup of coffee from the pot Connie had brewed that morning.

"The tricycle will be fixed quickly, I'm sure," she commented.

"But the two of them will need plenty of time to tease each other."

A Love Affair with Trains

Dad's love affair with trains began with a serious conversation at the age of eighteen.

"Chuck, you must get a job," his father, George, told him.

"I don't know what I want to do," Dad replied.

Because he struggled with math, Dad hadn't been able to complete the first year of high school. Perhaps he never envisioned a future for himself.

His father, a conductor with Southern Pacific Railroad, said, "Let me see if I can arrange an apprenticeship for you as a boilermaker."

So began a 30-year career in Dad's perfect job. After he had retired, David spotted the ideal phone for his grandpa—a long, green phone designed like a train.

"Thanks so much, David. I like this."

"Well, let's try it out," David said as he picked up his cell phone.

Dual blasts of "woo woo" echoed throughout the mobile home and everyone erupted in laughter. After several more phone calls, Dad agreed to disengage the ringer and rely on the extension phone to signal incoming calls.

I learned a group of young men were restoring an old steam locomotive. I knew Terry and called him.

"I heard you and some of your friends work on Saturdays to

restore one of the steam locomotives."

"Yes, it's a fascinating project."

"Well, I don't think you know that my dad worked for Southern Pacific for many years. He loves trains and is very interested in your project. Could I bring him down sometime to meet you and your buddies and see what you're doing?"

"Of course. Just bring him to the Brooklyn Roundhouse."

When I told Dad where we would meet Terry, he exclaimed, "The Brooklyn Roundhouse? That's where I worked on the boilers all those years."

Dad grew more excited as the day approached. We pulled into the parking lot and I retrieved Dad's walker from the trunk. He shuffled to the roundhouse.

I introduced him to Terry, who quickly got him acquainted with his friends. Immediately Dad stepped back in time to the days he loved.

"Hi, everybody. You know, I worked right here in these yards for thirty years. Now let me see what you've been doing.

"How much air pressure do you need here? What tool do you use to get up under there? I remember those difficult tight spots.

"You know, this 700 locomotive you're restoring was one of the special ones from my day."

I took pictures, capturing the unique blend of young and old train lovers. As we drove away, we both thought the adventure had come to an end.

About six months later Terry called Dad. "Hi, Charlie. We

finished restoring the 700. We've scheduled a celebration ride on Saturday through the City of Portland and up into Washington. I know you can't climb up into the car, but I thought you might want to wait on the sidewalk to see the 700 go by."

"You bet. What location would you suggest?"

Addi drove him to the designated spot. Although I couldn't be there to document the significant occasion, I imagined a grin spreading across his beaming face the moment he heard the whistle in the distance. Undoubtedly the crowd allowed him a front-row viewing spot and he waved to the conductor as the locomotive chugged down the track.

Word of his involvement with the restoration group reached the ear of a well-known producer of hour-long documentaries broadcast on a local TV station.

Sam called him one day. "Hey, Charlie, I heard you worked for Southern Pacific for many years. I wanted to do a special on trains and wondered if I could interview you."

"Sure. Glad to help you."

Sam's crew blended clips of locomotives traveling throughout the beautiful Colombia River gorge and the celebration ride of the refurbished locomotive. One of the segments included Dad in the roundhouse bantering with the guys about the trains and telling his story of how he became a boilermaker. His gift of gab and enjoyment of people made him a natural.

Periodically the local station would rerun the train documentary. Inevitably Dad would receive a call.

"Hey, Charlie, I saw you on TV yesterday."

He enjoyed his version of fame for many years.

Failing Health

Dad and Connie remained self-sufficient into their retirement years. When they needed additional help, Addi moved into their mobile home, occupying the second bedroom.

"OK, you two. What sounds good for dinner?" Addi, a fabulous cook like her mother, took over the main responsibility of cooking, with no argument from Dad.

As Connie's health needs escalated, Addi began sorting out her complicated medication. Dad lovingly cared for Connie during several serious illnesses.

"When Dave and I are overwhelmed with Mom's condition, and racing each other for the doorway, Grandpa is standing by Mom's bed, rubbing her arms and bending to kiss her," she said.

Several times Connie seemed too sick to survive, but then she would rally. Her grandson Don would call his wife Sandy at work. "It happened again. Mom called to say Grandpa got Grandma dressed today and they're headed for lunch at the senior center."

One night in 1993 Dad, Addi, and Addi's son David gathered around Connie's bed. Her labored breathing warned them this time she would not recover.

A Sacrificial Commitment

After Connie took her last breath Dad traipsed to the living room and lowered himself to the sofa letting his head drop into his hands.

Addi rushed to his side and put her arm around his shoulders. "Don't worry. I'll take care of you."

Determined he would never have to move from his home, Addi's commitment to Dad represented an amazing gift of love, compassion, comfort and security. Whenever I expressed my gratitude for her sacrifice, she'd respond, "Gail, this is my ministry so you can continue yours."

One day she told me, "You know, Gail, I've always viewed him as my father, never my stepdad." I felt pleasure knowing how much he meant to her. He had filled up empty spaces in her life beginning with her young adult years. Now at this stage of his life, she integrated her days with his to help them both move ahead.

Dad missed Connie deeply, but peace settled in my heart, because I knew he would still have a satisfying life. Though I lived in the Philippines our occasional phone visits kept us connected. Our hearts felt full every time we heard each other's voices.

During each furlough, we planned special outings and played cribbage together. He'd taught me to play, and we spent a lot of hours in his den competing with each other. Whenever the cards had been dealt and a smile spread across his face, I knew I would lose. But I didn't care. The love and attention he showered on me were his priceless gifts.

Zest for Life

Dad lived as full a life as possible. Monday through Friday he got himself ready for the day, fixed a simple breakfast, and waited for the bus at the bottom of his wheelchair ramp. He never missed a chance to go to the community center where he enjoyed a nutritious lunch and a visit with friends. His wavy white hair, bright eyes, and booming voice attracted attention. The group knew they could count on his friendly, encouraging words to make every newcomer feel welcome and eager to return.

He joined the wheelchair aerobics class after lunch or participated in the weekly handcraft class. Addi never knew what finished project he'd give her when he returned home. One of my treasures is a small glass bowl with colorful pieces of hand-torn paper glued to the outside.

Addi devised activities and ideas to help Dad maintain an active life and retain his independence. She listened and counseled, monitored the few medicines he took, rallied for justice if she felt he'd received unfair treatment, and loved him unconditionally. Her delicious cooking guaranteed his good health.

During one of our father-daughter conversations he told me, "I wake up every morning wondering what new person I'm going to meet and what new thing I'm going to learn."

Now I knew the secret of his zest for life. I felt proud to have him for my father and relished the time we spent together. I hoped I'd have him in my life for many more years.

"I'm shooting for 100," he'd tell his friends with a captivating grin. The family kept throwing significant birthday parties—80th, 90th, 95th. He willed himself to see the turn of the century in 2000 and won.

Shortly after his 97th birthday we overheard him say to a friend, "Well, I'm shooting for ninety-eight."

We were shocked. Did he know something we didn't?

Long Hospitalization

A few short hospital stays during Dad's lifetime hadn't slowed him down. His longer hospitalization in the summer of 2005, however, brought an unfamiliar result. Instead of discharging him to go home, the doctor transferred him to a rehab center where they hoped to restore his muscle strength. Though Addi had always fought against Dad being anywhere but home, she knew she had no choice this time.

Dad didn't like being confined, but he endeavored to make the best of his situation. His outgoing personality kicked into full gear each time someone entered his room.

"Come on in."

"Glad to see you."

"Have you heard my latest joke?"

"I remember when..." and he'd be off on a favorite story.

Since his mental capacities were in full working order—unlike most of the other patients—the hospital staff wandered into his room whenever they needed a pleasant and normal conversation. They nicknamed him "The Captain" because he regaled them with his stories.

He told me, "I can't seem to get my zip back. I'm trying my best because I want to go home."

One morning when I whizzed into his room I found him fully dressed and sitting in his wheelchair.

"Oh, hi, Dad."

"Hi, beautiful."

"Well, since you're over there I think I'll sit on your bed."

"Help yourself," he said cheerfully.

I plopped on his bed and stretched out my legs, ready to talk. Suddenly our conversation shifted to the topic of heaven. Words tumbled from his mouth.

"I told Connie, 'Stick around. I'm coming soon.'"

He smiled at the exciting prospect. My heart understood his eagerness, but I struggled with the ramifications of being left behind.

Greig had made two trips that year for a father-son visit. Addi told me that during one visit they had sat together in the den talking for four hours straight.

In early August my brother and I coordinated our flights to visit Dad together at the rehab center. We took pictures of each other with Dad and also with Uncle George, Dad's younger brother with whom he had reconciled at Connie's urging.

Only after returning to Orlando and reviewing my pictures did I realize how different Dad looked—fragile frame, sunken eyes, and expressionless face.

My mind drifted back to the way I'd kept my distance

throughout my college years. However, once I'd reunited with Dad, we established a different kind of father-daughter relationship. I recognized his endearing qualities and let go of my disappointment in his lack of involvement during my growing up years.

Saying Goodbye

In late September, I grabbed another block of time from work to fly to Portland for a week. I visited Dad every day.

One day I drove Addi to an appointment first and then we stopped at the hospital. Addi remained in the car while I hurried to Dad's room. His condition shocked me. He looked at me knowingly but couldn't form any words. The nurse and I fed him ice chips to moisten his dry mouth.

As I climbed back into the car, I could no longer deny the truth. These were his last days. Burying my head in my hands, I bent over the steering wheel and sobbed.

"I know nothing I say can lessen your sadness," Addi said as she lovingly patted my back. She added, "Last week, as we sat together in the lobby talking, I kept rubbing his arm. Somehow I knew that would be the last time I'd see him."

My call to Greig in the afternoon took him by surprise. He planned to visit in October.

"Greig, you need to come now."

He caught a red-eye flight the next evening, arriving in the early morning. Together we stood at Dad's side. His eyes were closed and he couldn't speak, but we sensed him listening as we talked softly. A tear dribbled down his cheek. We felt helpless but grateful we could both be there with him. Eventually Greig and I moved to nearby chairs to quietly visit with each other.

Frequently Greig would call out, "Dad, Gail and I are right here." Greig's tender way with Dad opened my eyes to his love for him.

After grabbing a light lunch at a nearby restaurant, we hurried back to his room. The head nurse intercepted us in the hallway. "It won't be long now," she said.

Our strong, cheerful, positive, lover-of-life Dad would soon leave us. We gazed at his peaceful face.

Suddenly Greig whispered, "I think he stopped breathing."

There'd been no struggle, no gasping. I remembered a favorite quote. "Our last breath on earth is followed by our next breath in heaven."

Greig and I will never forget that awesome moment. Neither of us cried. We accepted this as Dad's time. And we knew Connie had greeted him in heaven, completing their circle of love.

At the nurse's request, we wandered outside for a while. Leaning against the car, we silently pondered our Dad's amazing life.

"I'm glad it's a sunny day," Greig said.

The next weekend family members gathered for Dad's memorial service along with many friends from the mobile home court where he and Connie had lived for so many years. As different people shared, we laughed at memories of Dad's eccentric but endearing ways.

Before I left town, David sorted through Dad's tools and boxed up a few he thought Greig would appreciate. He knew they weren't ones Greig would use in his building business but would provide sentimental value.

"Hey, Greig did you receive the box David sent?"

"Yeah, you know I remember using that saw to make small cars with Dad when we lived on 36th street."

When loved ones are gone, the memory of things we did together and the words we exchanged live on.

I missed Dad deeply, realizing I'd never again hear his booming voice on the phone or feel the crush of his hugs. We'd built a close, loving relationship many daughters would envy. When I became willing to love Dad unconditionally, allowing his love to reach my heart and stepping forward to involve myself in his life, I finally saw the truth. He was a father who loved his daughter.

Dad died two months short of his 98th birthday. My earthly connection with him ended. Yet his legacy remained: his zest for life. If only I could follow in his footsteps.

UNEXPECTED SISTER

My heart ached without my father. But I found comfort in the relationship I enjoyed with Addi.

She hadn't always been a part of my life because we were born into different families. We met when her mother married my Dad. Addi was twenty-three and I was a college freshman living on campus. We both had one brother but no sister.

In the beginning we weren't close. I saw Addi occasionally during school breaks, but when my first job took me to California, I returned home only once a year. We'd see each other only if she happened to be at Dad and Connie's place when I visited.

Seven years later I moved to the Philippines. Addi wrote warm and friendly letters. I responded with daily happenings, but we did not have a deep personal connection.

My furloughs, which lasted several months, allowed time for more meals and activities with Dad and the family. Yet, I scheduled visits with them at my convenience and remained aloof and detached.

Gradually, as I observed Addi's personality and learned more about her life experiences, I became more comfortable with her. Her love, acceptance, and interest in my life drew me into a more open and meaningful friendship. We began spending hours sitting at the small table in the living room, laughing and talking together.

One day I shared something more personal than usual.

Leaning across the table, and resting her hand on mine, she said, "Gail, I like it when you confide in me."

Something clicked inside me. I realized I felt safe with her. She'd already become my friend, but in that moment I welcomed her into my heart as my sister—the sister I'd never had. God gave Addi to me as a gift. He used her to pull down the walls I had erected around my heart and push aside my fears.

The closeness we shared began filling empty spaces in our lives. Addi loved telling people, "You know, Gail and I are closer than most real sisters." Our relationship would provide the foundation we needed to face many difficult situations.

Eager to preserve our intimacy, we began exchanging long emails while I lived overseas and frequently talked by phone once I returned. Her love for life and for people always inspired me.

Unexpected News

One night I answered the phone and heard her sobbing. Eventually, in a soft voice, she announced, "The tests show I have colon cancer."

My heart lurched. No words surfaced to match her fear.

"Oh, Addi, I'm so sorry."

I listened while she explained details of the forthcoming surgery. I knew I must be at her side.

On the day of the surgery, I gathered in the dismal waiting room with Dad, David and Don, Don's wife Sandy, and two of Addi's close friends. Shifting anxiously in our chairs, we spoke few words. The hours inched by on the huge clock overhead.

Finally the doctor appeared. "I removed the tumor and some of Addi's colon." He added, "Her prognosis is good—complete recovery with no treatment needed."

We all breathed again.

Whenever I visited her hospital room, Addi never complained. The positive prognosis framed the plan for her future.

In spite of her pain, Addi's humor came through. Her voice had become raspy from the tube that had been in her throat during surgery, so she used a notepad to communicate.

"We need to give you another blood transfusion," a businesslike nurse announced one day.

Addi wrote, "Can you give me Italian blood? I've always wanted to sing."

Indignant, the nurse responded, "Oh, we don't differentiate here."

"It's a joke," Addi scribbled.

My schedule allowed me to remain in town for several weeks to help Addi recover. Knowing that cooking wasn't my expertise, Addi often offered cooking instructions from her bed. In the midst of her weakness, she thought of me.

When my departure drew near, David moved in to assume his mother's care. He cooked meals with ease, made his mom laugh, and filled a needful role without complaint.

Finally we were able to resume our "sister talks." Every time I heard her characteristic low voice and sweet greeting, "Hi, honey," I settled in for a delightful hour-long phone conversation. We teased, giggled, moaned at appropriate times, and related recent experiences to help bridge the distance between us.

Initially, her health grabbed a regular slot in our conversations. Gradually, the topic of cancer seldom cropped up. We trusted the doctor's decision to require no treatment. Our family continued to thank God for this blessing as we watched her become the old Addi and spread her contagious laughter.

One day, laughing at herself, she related a story about trying to care for her sons when they were both hospitalized following a serious motorcycle accident. David and Don dwarfed Addi's 5'2" stature.

"David became totally dependent on me. I tried the best I could, but maneuvering him in his wheelchair at his size was a real trick. One day while pushing him down the walkway, we hit a bump and he almost flew out of the wheelchair. We both got the giggles and couldn't stop.

"Another time I pushed Don down the hospital corridor, his injured leg protruding in front of him. I miscalculated a corner and ran him straight into the wall. Don screamed with pain and yelled, 'Mom, what are you doing?' I quickly found a nearby visitor and together we managed to wheel him back from the wall so I could turn him in the right direction."

Addi's health had now improved enough for her to return to work. She also resumed cooking, not only for Dad but for those in need—an ill neighbor, a tired new mother—and anyone who wandered into their home at meal time. Her gift of mercy opened people's hearts. She'd listen to them pour out their needs and spring into action to help them.

It's Back

Three years later, she went for her annual follow up. Expecting nothing unusual, I still looked forward to the report.

"It's back," she exclaimed. "My white blood count is elevated and the scan shows tumors in my liver and adrenal glands. The doctor thinks the cancer has metastasized. They'll do surgery to remove the tumors."

I froze. My heart screamed, *How could this be? The surgeon said he removed it all. Addi and I planned to grow old together.*

Later the doctor gently confirmed, "She's in Stage IV."

Dr. Yu suggested surgery as the next step. Addi agreed, eager to do whatever might help extend her life. After the surgery, Addi's daughter-in-law Sandy called me.

"The surgery didn't go the way we or the doctor anticipated," she reported. "As Dr. Yu prepared to remove the tumors in her liver and adrenal glands, he happened to look down toward her colon and noticed something suspicious. It turned out to be a cancerous mass wrapped around her colon. Using the allotted time, he removed the mass and more of her colon, but had to leave the tumors. Dr. Yu told us if he hadn't discovered that mass, Addi would have died from a strangulated colon within two weeks."

Later in the day, the doctor who assisted Dr. Yu in the

operating room stopped by Addi's hospital room. Unaware that Dr. Yu had not yet spoken to her, he looked down at Addi's pale face and apologized, "I'm sorry we weren't able to do more for you."

Immediately Addi knew the surgery had taken an unexpected turn. As soon as David and Don came, she asked them to tell her the whole story.

Afterwards, she said, "I'm grateful to be alive, but what about the tumors?" The realization the tumors were still in her body haunted her.

Dr. Yu couldn't speculate on a timeframe. "I'll only know how fast the cancer has grown after I get the results from the next scan."

I'd sent an urgent email message to my praying friends prior to the surgery. My friend Carol responded with a beautiful analogy that soothed my hurting heart.

Gardeners know the time to stake a plant is when it's small and slender, standing straight without a hint it would ever bend or break. That's when support is planned for, in the early days of tender, rapid growth that anticipates the winds it doesn't feel.

I will be a stake set beside you, to bolster you against the gales, a reminder you are in a growing place that brings turbulence and whirlwinds with it. I will be a stake that says you do not need to stand alone. I have prayed and trusted God to take you and Addi through the journey ahead. I don't yet know the outcome, but I do know God is in control, and He is Good All the Time! May the prayers of your friends bolster you and may you feel God's power, strength and perfect peace that passes all understanding.

My friend Carol pledged to be a stake beside me. Now I planted myself beside Addi to bolster, shelter, and shield her from feeling alone.

Addi had survived cancer for three years. Now she faced a battle for her life. Would she give up hope and choose to resign? Or would she walk forward in God's power, trusting Him to fight this battle for her? The choice was hers. I prayed and watched and waited.

An Exultant Walk

Addi chose to walk forward. She never entertained the option of giving up.

Taking the elevator to the second floor for her first chemo treatment, she entered the quiet and oppressive treatment area. No one in the room would have suspected the fear that must have gripped her heart.

"Hi, I'm Addi. What's your name?" she said as she turned to the woman next to her.

Soon gentle banter spread among the circle of patients tethered to their own IV poles.

During her weekly visits, Addi built a friendship with her new doctor, his assistants, and the nurses. They all looked forward to her appointments. Her friendliness and laughter broke through the gloomy atmosphere like a rainbow stretching across the sky after a heavy rain.

As the months marched on, she defied the odds. Dr. Maunder, her oncologist, named her his star patient.

"Addi, would you be willing to help me in the hospice program?"

"I'd love to."

"Well, after you feel better, we'll make our plan," he said.

The Tables Turn

When Addi and I first bonded as sisters, I filled the role of spiritual mentor. She drank in stories about God and His promises and grew in her perspective and knowledge of God.

I stood at her side as often as I could, eager to be her companion so she wouldn't feel alone as she went through chemo. She lost her hair, followed by mouth sores, rashes, cracked skin, and digestive challenges.

Still, she clung to her faith and maintained her habit of praying without ceasing. We watched God sustain her life and give her body the ability to endure all the ups and downs of her illness.

A new year ushered in an unexpected, but welcomed six-month remission. She took full advantage by cooking again for family and friends and venturing out on drives through the countryside with a neighbor. The scenery provided good medicine, but her favorite outing was the beach. She could hear the waves bathe the shore and feel the salt spray in her face.

The family dared to hope she would remain in remission. But, as summer drew to a close, Addi's blood tests revealed the cancer had returned, this time in her lungs. Weekly chemo appointments filled her calendar once again. After a couple of months, Addi's body began to show signs of decline.

At that point the tables turned. She became my spiritual teacher and modeled how to face suffering. Her spiritual perspective deepened and overpowered her physical condition. In those dark days she opened herself more fully to God, prayed constantly, and found solace and comfort in God's Word.

I felt privileged to sit at her feet and witness firsthand the incredible and loving way God ministered to her and drew her into a more intimate relationship with Him. With tenderness, God prepared her to live with Him in heaven.

One day she announced, "I'm so excited about going to heaven. I know God has work for me to do!"

I thought, *But heaven is a place to rest. Why wouldn't you long to rest after all the pain and struggles you've endured on earth?* I had to admit that some days, especially after a long work week of unending deadlines, I longed to rest in heaven. Not Addi. She loved to work and always looked for ways to help people. Her radiant countenance confirmed contentment and a genuine desire to leave her earthly home and work for God in heaven.

Another day she asked me, "What should I do when I see God? Shall I shake His hand—does He have hands? Or shall I hug Him—does He have shoulders?"

I laughed. "I don't know what you should do, but you will certainly know when that time comes."

She smiled. No fear, only anticipation of the glory to come. She became my mentor, my model, and my inspiration.

Family Memories

During a hospital stay in September 2007, Addi decided to discontinue chemo and begin hospice.

"In some ways I'm relieved to be off chemo," she told me during a phone call. "But the hospice nurse says I'm doing very well. Makes me wonder if I should go back on chemo."

Next thing I heard she had taken a side trip with David.

During one of my visits, someone slipped and revealed Dr. Maunder's prediction that she had only three months to live. With tears streaming down her pale cheeks, she relayed the news to me.

I found myself blurting out, "Well, God didn't say so."

Cupping my hand to my mouth, I hollered to the ceiling as if it were heaven, "Sorry, but she's not coming yet."

She laughed through her tears. November came and went. Addi was still with us.

By the beginning of December, she had continual pain from the cancer now lodged in her lungs. David gave her a drop of morphine twice a day. Rather than oxygen only at night, she now needed it throughout the day as well.

Aware of her deteriorating condition, we all prayed for her to last through Christmas. We longed for one more family celebration together.

Her brother Bernie arranged to spend a week with her prior to Christmas. She viewed this as a special gift from him, since he lived in Costa Rica and seldom visited the United States. He'd been supportive throughout her illness, but always from a distance. Now they would have their final conversations and hugs.

Prior to my visit I mailed Addi a letter in case something happened before my arrival. I wanted to "talk" to her one more time and say what I wanted her to hear.

Dear Addi,

I told you I felt sad you are experiencing pain and weakness. When you replied to me, 'Don't be sad,' I realized God is continuing to give you an anticipation of heaven. I can tell your increasing excitement is keeping you strong for this season of your life. It is hard to imagine all the wonders and joy you will experience whenever God takes you to His home.

I pray for God's strength for you, His courage to face each day, and His assurance He is holding your hand and walking each step with you. You continue to inspire me with your faith. I see God purifying your faith in this journey. Perhaps your trials are deepening your faith.

I'm looking forward to being there and sitting at your side while we tell each other more stories. You have an amazing story and I want to help you tell it to others.

See you soon, Sister. You are God's gift to me. I love you!

Addi hung on. After arriving, I focused on Addi and David. Putting up Christmas decorations never made it to my to-do list.

One day Addi's cousin Vicky came to the door, arms overflowing with bags of Christmas decorations.

"I thought you all needed to celebrate Christmas."

Brushing aside their misunderstandings and misconnections through the years, Vicky chose to bring joy to Addi.

As she watched Vicky turn the living room into a Christmas

wonderland, Addi perked up.

After helping, I said, "I have to run some errands. Need anything?"

"I don't think so," Vicky replied.

Later I learned they had talked about the past, forgiven each other and vowed to keep in touch. It took Addi's illness to create an opportunity and willingness for them to experience healing in their relationship.

In spite of Addi's weakness, we all agreed to carry out our Christmas Eve tradition of having dinner together. Don, Sandy and their children Nick and Lindsay arrived, with Sandy carrying her famous lasagna. Soon our stomachs were rumbling and our taste buds went on high alert as that wonderful Italian aroma wafted from the kitchen.

We'd decided not to exchange gifts. Being together represented the best gift any of us could give each other.

Camera in hand, I sought to preserve memories of what we knew would be our last holiday together. With her oxygen tube well positioned around her nose and her familiar blue velour bathrobe covering her appropriately, Addi posed for pictures. Her blue eyes twinkled with joy as she laughed and hugged her children and grandchildren.

Christmas Day dawned. Though Addi didn't feel as well as she had on Christmas Eve, she insisted Don and the family still come over. We all wanted to be together for her December 25 birthday. God had fulfilled her desire to make it to the age of seventy.

Remembering Addi

I hoped for another chance to talk to Addi. She'd been too weak to talk by phone throughout January. And the morphine caused hallucinations which prevented understandable conversations. I missed our sister talks and felt far away and disconnected.

At the end of Don's work week, he'd stop by the apartment to relieve David. Both of them had time to sit with their mother, saying their goodbyes and expressing their love.

One evening I dialed Addi's number to get an update. Expecting to hear David or Don's voice, I was shocked when Addi answered.

"Hi Addi. I'm so glad to hear your voice. How are you today?"

After a little catching up, she said, "I wish you were my neighbor."

How I wish I had thought to say, "I will be your neighbor soon". We'd always talked about having mansions next to each other in heaven. We'd had many opportunities to be together in the last years, relating the latest thing we'd learned about God, marveling at His faithfulness, and laughing about unforgettable adventures we'd had. We missed each other. After no conversation for more than a month, God had created a window of time for us to talk again that day. I felt less lonely.

Arriving home from work two days later, I pressed the button to retrieve my messages.

"Gail, this is David. The hospice nurse says it won't be long."

Sadness crackled in his voice. How I wished I could hug him and sit with him.

Several hours later, the phone rang again.

"Mom passed away." This time his voice sounded calm. "I'd been sitting by her bed. Then I sat out on the porch for a few moments where I could see her through the window. After a few moments I realized I didn't see her breathing."

Rushing in, he had stood at her bedside and realized she was gone. The mother who had been there for him his entire life defied the odds and survived for two and a half years with Stage IV cancer. She'd fought a courageous battle. Though brokenhearted, he knew she was now at peace with God.

Her memorial service became a celebration of life. At her request, I'd written a list of what she wanted in her service, including the doctors she wanted me to invite to participate. She asked me to speak also.

"Addi, I don't know if I'll be able to do that. I will miss you so much."

"Honey, I would really like you to because I know it will be so meaningful."

"OK."

In a last gesture of love she dictated a letter to those who would gather for her service. I placed it on the inside page of the memorial folder that each person could take home.

TO ALL MY FAMILY AND FRIENDS

How do I express my love for all of you, for the wonderful way I have been treated, the love from each and every one of you, and the love I have been able to return to you.

I've had the gift of God since early childhood, and He has played an incredible role in all of my life, through all the ups and downs. Were it not for Him I would not be where I am today, but with all of the gifts I have had in my life, my family, my friends, and my foster children, God is my greatest gift. As the old saying goes, "I'm at the last roundup, and I am excited about it."

I love all of you. I am going to miss you and you are going to miss me, but life goes on. We will see what God has in store for me in heaven.

I love you,

Addi Farley

Her chiropractor, Dr. Billy Flowers, spoke concluding his remarks with, "Addi was the most amazing person I've ever met."

Dr. Dick Maunder, because of an out-of-town commitment, sent a letter for the pastor to read.

I was continually inspired by Addi's zest for life and her ability to be guided by hope. In her moments of greatest distress, she still had a smile on her face and a capacity to care for others around her.

Addi was very much a people person. She cared for and about others. Relationships were everything to her. At our visits, she always inquired about my family. She was one of a handful of patients who always called me by my first name.

After developing cancer, she started beating the medical odds, outliving all the predictions of her physicians. And her last miracle, although it's hard for us to see it that way, became the final healing and relief of suffering she experienced as her life in that broken body came to a close.

I am grateful for the legacy Addi leaves. She was truly a role model for all of us. And the advice she leaves for us is this: To live simply, yet abundantly; to look for the good in everything and everyone; to hope; to believe in miracles; and to love everything about life.

We will miss you, dear friend.

Then Nick and Lindsay shared the podium. With their words they painted a beautiful picture of their grandmother, including all the ways they would miss her. Unable to play the song "I Can Only Imagine," Lindsay read some of the words instead.

My turn came next. God knew what Nick and Lindsay were going to say and He wove our words together. As I concluded my planned remarks, I looked at them and smiled.

"I can only imagine the scene when Addi met God face to face for the first time."

Addi had wondered what she should do in that moment. I'm sure her uncertainty vanished the moment she saw God standing with outstretched arms, beckoning her to come to Him so He could welcome her home.

David cried quietly during the service. Sitting beside him, I tried to console him, as did his long-time friend who leaned forward from behind us to place her hand on Dave's trembling shoulder.

At the end of his prayer, the pastor said to the audience, "This may be a time to reflect. Or perhaps you need to forgive. Maybe you need to say you're sorry. Or maybe you need to let go."

During this time I sensed that Dave began letting go of his mother. And I saw evidence during the reception. Usually aloof in social situations, he talked with people, smiled, laughed and appeared very comfortable. Several family members commented, "Dave seems so different today."

Because Addi gave each of us her gifts of love, laughter, and friendship, we would never be the same.

FILLING EMPTY SPACES

One evening, soon after returning from Addi's memorial service, I propped myself on my comfy blue couch. Grateful to be back in my quiet condo, I gazed at the four pictures adorning my coffee table. Mom beaming while preparing Christmas candles. Dad smiling after winning a game of cribbage. Addi grinning during a family gathering.

My eyes shifted to the picture of my brother, his arm draped around my shoulder during a recent visit. "Greig, you'd better not leave me." I said aloud. "We're the only ones left." I smiled to myself. *That shouldn't happen for a while. We're both still young.*

Childhood Pal

I adored my older brother. My parents adopted him soon after he was born. Thrilled with their first child, my parents named him Greig, which was the maiden name of Dad's mother. She had given it to my father by naming him Charles Greig; now he passed it to his new son.

Mom and Dad had ventured into the adoption process because they believed they were unable to have children. However, eleven months later Mom gave birth to me. She said she felt like she was raising twins, and her work expanded when she had to keep track of us as toddlers. For me it meant having a childhood pal.

51

We played together constantly. Sledding down the steep street in front of our house, when city officials blocked it off during winter snows, rated high on our list of favorite things to do.

In contrast to my cautious nature, Greig embraced adventure. Before his seventh birthday he climbed onto the roof of our neighbor's house. Everything proceeded according to his plan until a misstep hurled him to a sharp rock below. Blood gushed from his right check. The owners saw him sail past their window and ran to tell my parents who rushed him to the hospital. His scar remained as proof of his adventurous spirit, a trait that would become more obvious in the ensuing years.

While we were still young, our parents moved to a larger home. Greig devised a creative croquet course that traveled across our expansive back yard, continued through the concrete alleyway between the house and garage, and ended with the last wicket perched between the uneven roots of the tree on the parking strip. Of course, Greig could always hit his ball through that precariously-positioned wicket and win the game.

As he grew older, the apple tree in one corner of our backyard beckoned to him. Soon he and Dad erected a simple tree house. I thought Greig planned it as another place for us to play together. Soon it became apparent he viewed it as forbidden territory—for boys only.

Uncharacteristically defiant, I convinced my girlfriend Beverly to climb up the tree house with me one day to check out the view. As we plopped down on the wooden boards, feeling smug and victorious, I heard a rustle.

Jerking to attention, I peered over the side and spotted Greig scowling below, arms folded across his chest. "Hey, what are you two doing up there? You know it's off limits."

Cowering, I turned to Beverly, "Yikes, we'd better get out of here."

Different Roads

Though Greig still took the protective-brother stance whenever he thought someone treated me unfairly, our relationship began to shift. During high school, we chose different lifestyles and followed separate paths.

While we would always be bound as brother and sister, I'm not sure we ever understood each other. I often asked myself, *Why is Greig acting that way?* Undoubtedly he viewed me as his naïve, passive sister.

Many years later, as I reflected on our separate lives, I made a shocking discovery. Greig and I battled the same fear—the fear of rejection—but we chose different routes to overcome our fear. Greig became defiant, I became compliant. His path led to alcoholism; mine to perfectionism.

I remained in our family structure to try to achieve my goal of acceptance. Greig roamed a different road seeking love, acceptance and belonging from alcohol, pretending he didn't care what the family thought of him.

Greig drank to cover up his fear, to blot out the pain and

disappointments of life. I fought my fear by striving for perfection and excellence. We both longed for affirmation to prove we were loved and accepted.

Not receiving verbal affirmation except from my grandmother, I kept trying to earn it. In the process, I became what everyone else wanted. No one knew the real me, an insecure and fearful person. My well-positioned mask and high standard of performance earned me external acceptance but held my heart in bondage.

I moved to California for my first job. Greig worked in Portland for a while, and then helped with the pipeline project in Alaska before heading off to Colorado where he set up a residential and commercial construction business.

Porter Construction became well known throughout the area. Greig and his crews built million-dollar country clubs and palatial homes on snowy slopes. Greig's reputation as a builder seemed unbeatable. But his alcoholism competed. Mom knew how much he struggled, but kept the details from the rest of us.

One day mother received a call from Greig. Fortunately, he had good news to tell her.

"Hi, Mom. Wanted you to know Carol and I got married."

Though disappointed there'd been no official wedding to share in, she felt relieved. Now, she thought, he has someone in his life who will give him the love and understanding he needs.

Greig and Carol welcomed their first child, Jake. They were delighted when their second son Casey joined the family a couple years later. The four of them enjoyed skiing the slopes of the Colorado Rockies together. From the time they were young, the boys always loved riding motorcycles like their dad. Years later Greig Sterling, always known as Buster, was born into the family. At an early age, he joined in all the favorite outdoor activities.

Carol thought Greig's drinking was behind him. When it surfaced again, he went into rehab. This helped for a time, but his weakness for alcohol still taunted him.

Shared Identity

Though my parents had adopted Greig when he was only a few days old, and had given him a family name, he wrestled with a sense of abandonment. He'd never admitted it, but in moments of personal reflection I recognized those feelings in his pattern of life.

God began unfolding His plan by sending someone into his life who could identify with Greig's sadness of abandonment and absence of love. Someone he had abandoned unknowingly when she was born. A daughter named Regan.

Regan's mother, only seventeen when she gave birth, entrusted Regan's care to her own mother. Regan called her Grandmother "GrandMom". Eventually Regan's grandparents adopted her as their own daughter.

As a wife and mother of two children, Regan experienced deep, emotional turmoil in her heart. She'd never known her real father. Desperately longing for his love, she began to search for him.

Regan's biological mother and her GrandMom gave her the

scant information they knew about Greig and his family. After uncovering a few more facts, she began calling through the Porters in the phone book. One day she called Charles Porter. My dad answered the phone.

"Hello. I wanted to ask if you are Gail's father."

"Yes."

"Are you Greig's father?"

"Yes."

Knowing she'd found the right person, she announced, "I believe I am Greig's daughter."

That day I received a phone call from Addi. Fortunately I happened to be on furlough from the Philippines. She invited me to meet her for lunch the following day.

Once we were seated she said, "We received an interesting phone call yesterday from a young woman who says she is Greig's daughter. She's married with two small children and lives nearby. We invited her to come for a visit tomorrow afternoon. Can you join us?"

"Wow, what a shock. Of course, I'll be there."

Regan brought her adorable son AJ and energetic daughter Anjela. Connie, Addi, and I welcomed her as family. Regan conversed easily. Dad took a while longer to adjust to the shock.

We gave Greig's address and phone number to Regan. She wrote him a letter, which stunned him. He'd been told that Regan's mother didn't have the baby. Now he faced a dilemma. Was she really his child? If she were, did he want to let her into his life?

Carol encouraged him to respond to Regan's letter and invite her to fly out and meet all of them. As soon as they saw each other at the airport they experienced an immediate connection.

Quickly they developed a father-daughter relationship. Regan's success in finding Greig allowed them to build the kind of relationship neither of them had experienced before, a relationship built on unconditional love and acceptance.

For the next twenty years they tried to make up for all the time they had lost. They lived on opposite coasts, but Greig scheduled all kinds of outdoor adventures for them—skiing, boating, and hiking. Sometimes those adventures involved only the two of them, but most often it included one or all of her newfound brothers, Jake, Casey, and Buster. Carol accepted her into the family and they developed a friendly relationship.

No Safety Net

Greig's alcoholism continued to haunt him and eventually led to his and Carol's divorce. He stayed in touch with the three boys. He and Carol continued making decisions as co-parents for their youngest son Buster. During his high school years and beyond, Buster lived with his dad.

After our mother's death Greig's life plummeted. His safety net had disappeared forever. He floundered and became afraid of life without her. She was a special, caring, yet enabling mother—like many mothers of alcoholics.

Mother's absence from his life created cracks in Greig's well-defended resistance to God. Gradually Greig began a spiritual search. God knew it would take the pain of our mother's death to create a willingness in his heart to consider God.

Greig turned toward me, asking questions about God. Later I would realize he'd always kept himself at a distance from me because of my love of God and his fear that God wouldn't accept him because of all he'd done.

When he started searching, God began building a bridge for Greig to find Him. Occasionally he phoned me in the Philippines. New vulnerability surfaced during our phone conversations, and his spiritual questions amazed and thrilled me. He seemed to have detoured on his road to destruction.

In February of 1990, Greig wrote a letter containing encouraging news.

Well, since Christmas a lot of things have changed around here. First and foremost I haven't been drinking, not a <u>drop</u>. December 26 I went to visit a friend in New York. My friend also has a drinking problem, but unlike me has been able to resist the temptation to pick up a drink. He says he has found the power to resist in God. How about that! I'm very sure that's no surprise to you. As it turns out, he was good company for me, as I quit drinking and believe I am finding the power, the ability to keep away from drinking, in God as well. Amazing for me to be saying something like this, isn't it? Oh well, I hope I'll keep the <u>power</u> if you know what I mean. So far so good!

In July his second letter arrived. Again he talked about his "new personal direction." He continued, "I'm feeling everything will turn out for the best. That would be a bit of my new outlook and higher power shining through."

Two years later I received a letter from his best friend Richard, a co-worker he'd known for many years. Richard, his wife Sandy, and their three daughters enjoyed spending time with Greig, Carol and their sons. In his letter, Richard confirmed Greig's change.

I am happy to tell you that, I believe, he has been released from his problem, at least for now. He seems serious about putting things back in order.

The next year Richard updated me. *By all appearances Greig has made an extraordinary recovery from the dark times of last fall.*

Reunited on the East Coast

Greig lived in a small town in South Carolina when I moved back from the Philippines to work at Campus Crusade's International Headquarters in Orlando. Since we were only a five-hour drive apart, we visited each other occasionally in addition to our regular phone calls. Our adult friendship flourished.

From Greig's comments I knew he still struggled with alcoholism from time to time. He didn't seem as open to God as he had after visiting his friend in New York several years before. But I didn't give up. I remembered the Apostle Paul's explanation in 1 Corinthians 3:6-7, "I planted, Apollos watered, but God was causing the growth. So then neither the one who plants nor the one who waters is anything, but God who causes the growth."

I also claimed the promise of Philippians 1:6, "For I am confident of this very thing, that He who began a good work in you will perfect it until the day of Christ Jesus."

Greig began to talk about Glenn, a coworker in the same construction company. They shared camaraderie and the same high standard of excellence. Glenn lived by his Christian faith. Greig noticed.

One morning after one of Greig's longest binges, Glenn wrestled with a burden for him. While driving to work he sensed God saying to him, "Write a letter and take it to Greig's house."

Glenn drove to the office. Sitting at his desk he poured out his heart to Greig in a handwritten letter. He knew where Greig lived, having visited him several times.

Knocking on the door and receiving no response, he tried the door. It was unlocked. Walking inside he saw Greig sprawled on his couch.

"Greig, it's Glenn," he said as he quickly knelt on the floor.

"Glenn, I'm not in very good shape."

"I can see that," he said gently.

They talked for a little while.

Then Glenn asked, "Greig, what do you want?"

"I want what you have."

"You can have it," Glen said.

Later Greig read me Glenn's letter, a letter full of love and acceptance and an explanation of how he could know Jesus. His heart's door opened some more. Soon afterwards Greig agreed to visit Glenn's church. Glenn and his wife Jackie showered Greig with love.

One Sunday, while sitting together in church, Greig heard the pastor's invitation to come forward and accept Jesus. Jackie, sitting beside him, grabbed his hand. Greig didn't resist. He followed Jackie and Glenn to the altar where he prayed a prayer of acceptance.

After Greig explained his experience to me, I asked him what he had prayed that day.

"I said I accepted Jesus Christ as my Savior and Lord," Greig replied.

"Great prayer," I assured him.

His life began to change as he continued to attend church and became acquainted with some church members who were also builders. Glenn continued to befriend Greig and kept me informed of Greig's progress and setbacks.

True Brother and Sister

One night the phone rang.

"Hi Gail."

"Oh, Greig, how are you?"

"Not doing so well tonight."

One moment he wallowed in self-pity because of his drinking. The next moment he expressed a desire to change his life and be free.

"Greig, you know only God can give you the power to change."

Usually he closed out our conversation after this kind of reminder, but this time he continued.

"I don't want this kind of life anymore," he said.

"Are you willing to let God give you a different kind of life?" I asked.

"Yes."

I told him God loved him and wanted to have a personal relationship with him.

"You can begin your personal relationship by talking with God. Do you want to pray?"

"Yes."

Following me phrase by phrase, he repeated a prayer of acceptance of Jesus. God kept me calm, though I wanted to shout with joy.

Afterwards Greig said, "That prayer sure was a better one than mine would have been."

"It doesn't matter the words you say. God knows your heart."

As we continued our phone conversation, I heard a knock at the door. Carrying the phone with me, I opened the door and saw my friend Ella who knew all about Greig's situation. I motioned her inside and mouthed, "It's Greig."

Soon she realized our conversation had turned to eternal life and life in heaven. I grinned at her. I knew she was praying for our conversation.

I explained to Greig that the day we accept Christ becomes our spiritual birthday.

"Your spiritual birthday was probably the day you accepted Christ at Glenn and Jackie's church."

"Well, to make sure, let's say it's today," he quipped.

"OK. Then June 17, 2004 is your spiritual birthday."

Though a new concept to him, I could tell the thought pleased him.

As we finished I said, "Now we will both see Mom in heaven."

When our mother died, he knew without a doubt she was in heaven. Now, in God's timing, he had a secure place in heaven because he had allowed Jesus to come into his heart.

We promised to talk again soon. When I finished our call, Ella and I prayed together that God would preserve the seed He'd planted in Greig's heart so Satan could not snatch it away, and that Greig's faith would grow.

Later I mailed him a simple certificate declaring, "June 17, 2004. Greig Porter's Spiritual Birthday." From time to time I referred to his spiritual birthday.

Immediately he'd add with a lilt in his voice, "Yes, June 17."

Now we were in the same spiritual family, true brother and sister, both assured of our heavenly Father's love forever. Our relationship deepened.

One day Greig said, "I'll never be like you."

"Good," I replied. "God doesn't want you to be. He has His own special plan for you. I'm a missionary this way, but I believe God wants you to help others who have experienced some of the same things you have."

"We'll see," he said.

He always remembered to call me on my birthday. One year my birthday came and went without a call. I wondered. The next evening, after returning from work, I pressed the button to retrieve my messages. A familiar voice rang out.

"Hi, Gail. This is your brother. Wanted to call and wish you a happy birthday—well, happy birthday and one day that is. When I turned over my calendar this morning I said, 'Oops!' Anyway I hope everything is fine with you and you had a good day. Everything is good here."

He began giving me brotherly advice about household problems as well as personal situations. We'd become partners and encouraged each other.

Startling Diagnosis

In August of 2009, at the end of a family visit in Portland, Casey called me.

"Aunt Gail, I wanted to let you know Dad is in the hospital and they think he has leukemia."

My world changed in a day. Greig's did, too.

A daily runner for exercise, and a builder who constantly climbed up and down ladders and maneuvered heavy machinery, Greig enjoyed excellent health. An outdoorsman, he loved skiing, cycling, hang gliding, deep sea diving, water skiing, and driving his boat through the many waterways of the beautiful low country of South Carolina.

Earlier that summer Richard and Sandy had driven up from

Lakeland, Florida for a short visit. They talked, laughed, ate, and boated. Later Richard told me, "Greig mentioned he felt quite tired, but we had a great time."

His unusual fatigue became obvious when he tried to cover the full course of his usual morning run and could only make it halfway. He had to pause and rest halfway up the ladder at work sites and felt exhausted walking ten yards to his mailbox and back.

When He took his blood pressure, the monitor showed 90/40. His online research led him to believe this indicated only a blood pressure problem.

As a new member of Medicare, he could have one free annual exam. He scheduled an appointment with Dr. Perez for Thursday. Saturday morning the phone rang.

"Hello, Greig. This is Dr. Perez. I'm at a medical conference in California but my office called me with the results of your blood test. It is indicative of leukemia. You need to go to the ER now. I'm making arrangements at Hilton Head Regional Medical Center."

"Would it be OK if I checked in on Monday? I have a few things to take care of," Greig said.

"Sorry, but you need to go now."

Alarmed, he relayed the news to his son Buster. As a prospective employee of a trucking company, Buster needed to drive to Texas that day for a training class and couldn't drive him to the hospital. Uncertainty lingered around them like stale air. They said a few parting words and hugged goodbye.

Extremely fatigued yet fiercely independent, Greig climbed

into his own car for the thirty-minute drive to the hospital. He checked in and waited. Finally he heard his name called.

After a series of routine questions, the doctor studied his test results.

"With such low blood pressure, we are amazed you could drive here. Most people would be crawling on the floor."

The doctor continued, "Your results show you have AML, which is acute myeloid leukemia. Unfortunately, our hospital is unable to give you the aggressive treatment you need. We are arranging for an ambulance to transport you to Memorial Health Hospital in Savannah. Dr. Lewis is an excellent oncologist and he will oversee your care."

Greig knew he had no choice.

At the Savannah hospital, medical personnel transported Greig to his room where he endured eight days of twenty-four-hour chemo treatments. Then he waited.

Each day Dr. Lewis visited his room, reporting his counts. He could only release him once the leukemia cells dropped to 1 percent.

Journey in Georgia

Two days after arriving home from Portland, I packed my car and headed toward the freeway for my five-hour drive to the Savannah hospital. After a couple of phone conversations with Greig during the trip, I pulled into the hospital parking garage.

Eager to see him, but uncertain what to expect, I wound my way to the isolation ward. After washing my hands at the sink outside his room, I pushed the door open.

Hearing someone, he rolled over and smiled. "Hi Gail."

"Hi Greig." I bent down to hug him, relieved to see him.

He lay connected to the IV. But rather than a hospital gown, he wore khaki shorts and a mauve T-shirt. His beautiful gray hair framed his handsome, tan face.

I lowered myself to the closest chair. He started talking about all that had happened and outlined Dr. Lewis's plan.

"I'm so glad I can be here with you. I'll be able to stay a couple of weeks."

At the end of the evening Casey and his wife Jessica arrived for a short visit before leading me to Greig's house. It had been many years since I'd had a lengthy visit with Casey and had not yet met Jessica.

As the three of us prepared to leave, Greig said, "Now, Gail, remember I want you to sleep in my room." The love and care his words conveyed touched me.

Though late when we left the hospital, I treated Casey and Jessica to dinner. Serious circumstances had brought us together, but we relished the chance to visit not only as relatives but as three friends who needed each other.

Afterwards, Jessica climbed into my car. Grateful for their guidance in unfamiliar territory, I followed Casey through the back roads to Greig's house in Bluffton. Casey carried my bag inside and made sure I felt comfortable staying there alone.

"We'll come and get you in the morning so we can ride to the hospital together. Is 10:00 good for you?"

The next morning I awoke to quietness, grateful for the night's sleep. Padding into Greig's kitchen, with its cozy round oak table and chairs, I welcomed the sun shining through two large windows. I looked across the grass to the sprawling oak tree and pondered what lay ahead in this unexpected journey.

Continuing Care

Greig felt comfortable in Dr. Lewis's care. During his daily rounds, he and Greig bonded. Though sick and facing inevitable side effects, Greig never lost his humor. He remained pleasant and cooperative.

His positive reputation with the medical personnel cut through protocol. They enjoyed popping into his room, whether they were assigned to him that day or not. Occasionally when one of his favorite nurses pulled the night shift, she called ahead to ask what he felt like eating and made a detour to a drive-through on her way to work. Those caring gestures encouraged Greig and created bright spots during the long days.

The waiting and observation period stretched into fifty days. We were grateful for Medicare coverage, which took effect only three months prior to Greig's diagnosis.

Though battling side effects, and what Greig called "chemo brain," he still kept tabs on Harley, the dog he loved. We all tried to relate cute and funny stories of Harley's antics when we visited. Soon Greig began saying he wanted to see Harley. I kept putting off his request, not wanting to deal with the logistics.

One day, with a scowl on his face, Greig raised his voice and demanded, "I want to see Harley."

I knew I could no longer avoid it. The master had spoken. He needed to see his companion.

Casey and I figured out a day he and Jessica could bring Harley. Greig and I conspired about how to sneak Harley up to the room. Confident the plan would be foiled, we planned to meet them outside.

As usual, I worried about the risk of germs from the people he'd see and the air he'd breathe. His excitement as he laced up his running shoes overpowered my fears.

Casey and Jessica arrived with Harley and a cup of Greig's favorite ice cream. As soon as Harley spotted Greig he ran to him. Greig's delight as he bent down to hug him made the risk worth it.

The blazing sun prompted Greig and Casey to seek refuge on a grassy spot under a small tree to enjoy their ice cream. As I looked at father, son, and beloved dog crouched together, smiles of pure delight covering their faces, happiness poured over my soul. How I wished I would have had my camera to record that priceless moment.

Occasionally, when I had time at the house before or after a hospital visit, I'd stroll down Greig's street toward the river at the end of the road. The country atmosphere, with its picturesque wooden fences and horse pastures, soothed my spirit. I drew confidence for the uncertain days ahead as God assured me He would hold my hand as we walked through the valleys and climbed treacherous mountain paths.

Father-Daughter Time

In late August Regan flew out to be with her Dad for a couple of weeks. Her visit became a balm to his spirit. She sat at his bedside, monitored the reports from Dr. Lewis, and lent creative advice for an easier way to climb into bed now that the chemo had weakened his body.

As the time of her departure neared, I drove back up to South Carolina to see her. We visited Greig together on her last morning.

Dr. Lewis walked into the room for his rounds and smiled. "Greig, you have responded well to the treatment and the leukemia cells are now less than 1 percent. Let's talk about the next step. I recommend a second, less severe round of chemo in preparation for a bone marrow transplant. The best place for this transplant to happen is at the Medical University of South Carolina in Charleston. I have spoken to Dr. Stuart, a well-known oncologist who has a great team. They will call you for an appointment."

Fortunately, Regan could hear the news directly from Dr. Lewis. We rejoiced, but we knew Greig faced a very long journey.

In preparation for Greig's release, Casey, Jessica and their two-year-old daughter Piper moved into Greig's home to help him. We were glad Greig could be home, but his energy never returned. Unsteady on his feet, he spent most days on the couch.

Charleston Experiment

His next blood analysis showed the leukemia cells had increased again. Dr. Stuart and his team had planned for the less severe treatment prior to a transplant, but after seeing the blood tests, they decided to repeat the same aggressive treatment to immediately attack the leukemia cells.

Without further treatment Greig would die soon. Yet another severe eight-day, twenty-four-hour round of chemo could move him into the 25 percent category of patients who do not survive. Greig still answered, "I'm willing."

He returned to the hospital. Doctor Stuart no longer discussed a bone marrow transplant. First, he wanted to see if Greig would survive the chemo.

Because of the severity of what lay ahead, Greig was attentive when God opened an opportunity for me to talk to him about the commitment he had made to Jesus.

"I've observed changes in you since June 17, 2004," I said. "I am confident no matter what happens to you, you will live in heaven forever."

"Thanks for telling me that. It encourages me."

"God will be with you each step of the way. None of this is a surprise to God."

We both knew if he didn't survive, he had the assurance of eternal life in heaven with God. That's what mattered to us.

Unusual Christmas Gift

Greig survived the second round of chemo. The doctor then started the process of finding a bone marrow match, the only cure for his AML.

Twelve million people had signed up as worldwide bone marrow donors, yet the registry did not guarantee a perfect or acceptable match. Two perfect matches were located immediately.

On December 23 God gave Greig an early Christmas gift: an infusion of bone marrow flown in from the donor in Germany.

During the first week Greig suffered severe digestive problems, which doctors thought may have been brought on by the eight days of chemo.

Dr. Stuart told me, "His system has to hit bottom before it can spring to life again."

My friends and I prayed that Greig's body would accept the donor's bone marrow and his new immune system would begin producing healthy cells. Soon tests showed a positive result.

After his release, he'd be required to stay in the Charleston area for at least two months for daily blood tests as an outpatient. Due to winter rates, we were able to rent an old condo on Folly Beach at a cheap rate. We both looked forward to shifting from the hospital to the beach.

Recovery at the Beach

Greig called less than a month after the transplant. "Hey, Gail. Dr. Stuart says I can be released and go to Folly on Tuesday."

"Oh, wow. Wonderful news. Unfortunately, I have some work deadlines this week and won't be able to come until Thursday. Will that be OK?"

"I'll explain your situation to them."

The list of things Greig wanted from his house expanded each time he called. Thursday arrived and so did one more phone call. "It's going to be cold," Greig said, "so bring my heavy jacket, and the black knit hat and black leather gloves from my dresser. Oh, and bring Harley's leash from the back porch."

After packing things at his house, I pulled into town. Driving to the front of the hospital, I left the car and hurried to the fifth floor.

As I pushed open the door, I saw a nurse showing paperwork to a man. I paused, thinking the short-haired man in light colored pants and a white long-sleeved shirt was the doctor. Suddenly I realized it was Greig. He looked healthy and normal. He chuckled later when I told him my first reaction.

As Greig and I drove away, with our belongings filling the back seat, I couldn't believe we were finally headed to his "recovery station".

Both of us took the first load up the stairs to the sixth-floor condo. At each landing we stopped to gaze at the beach.

Once inside, Greig sat on the couch and said, "Gail, I'm really sorry but I don't think I can help you bring up any more things. I'm really tired."

"No problem, Greig. I'll get the rest. I'm glad we're here."

Once I'd completed my trips to the car, we stood side by side at the window. The waves crashed on the shore and the weathered pier marched out to the ocean. The balcony would allow Greig to sit outside when he didn't feel like walking on the beach.

Greig rested a lot. One morning I wandered out to the front room but didn't see Greig lying on the couch. Harley was missing as well. Soon I heard footsteps on the stairs. In walked Greig, bundled up in his winter clothes, with Harley close behind. He had climbed up and down six flights of stairs for his morning walk. Hope rose in my heart.

We settled into a morning routine of driving to the hospital for blood tests, followed by Greig's nap when we returned. My role included monitoring bills, organizing the blood result sheets, sorting the various packets of medicine according to the time of day needed, and increasing my skill in cleaning his port each day. We were both ready to watch TV by the time we'd eaten dinner.

In my desire to fulfill these daunting responsibilities, I maintained a calm manner around Greig. He often thanked me, which I appreciated. But alone in my room, anxiety filled my heart and tears flowed. Am I doing a good job, I wondered. Greig had already offered to take over the chore of cleaning his port since my hands shook each time. God reminded me He would continue to equip me for this part of the journey.

Inner Character

Being with my brother on a continuing basis opened my eyes to the special person he'd become and the way he lived his life. I felt so proud of him.

Greig's reputation as an excellent builder was well known everywhere he lived because he set high standards. He pursued his passion with diligence, to the point of putting finishing touches on the work of sub-contractors to insure excellence.

He handled finances with integrity and kept his paperwork very organized. The files I'd brought with me from his house had distinct and logical labels. He'd established systematic procedures for paying bills on time. As a willing assistant, I desired to keep everything in the same neat and orderly manner until he returned to normal life and could take charge again.

No longer a victim of life circumstances, he'd become a happy, kind, caring, and compassionate person who enjoyed meeting other people's needs. During his first hospitalization he asked us to bring his drafting tools and sketch pad so he could draw a proposal for an extra room one of his nurses wanted to add to her home.

Greig had become a favorite patient at the hospital. His humor relaxed the nurses. His cooperative and positive spirit lessened the weight of the doctor's difficult work. Many times after conversing with him as their patient, they shifted their conversation to personal topics.

He and another patient, Frank, developed a friendship when they learned they both had AML. Once they were released, they

75

compared progress reports whenever they showed up for blood work at the same time.

A Caring Friend

I'd been in town for several weeks of Greig's recovery when Buster arrived to be with his dad for the weekend. That night Richard arrived to take over caregiving so I could travel to India for a work project.

Greig and Buster left to see a movie while Richard stayed behind to learn the procedure for sorting out and keeping tabs on the various medications. Fortunately, Greig had taken over the chore of cleaning out his port. Richard called this part of Greig's journey the "road to recovery".

I hated to leave, but as predicted, Richard and Greig enjoyed guy talk, laughed at memories from more than twenty years of friendship, and planned for Greig's future.

Expecting they would be together for several more weeks, I was caught off guard when I received Richard's email after returning from India. He told me Dr. Stuart had released Greig to return to his home and allowed him to come for weekly instead of daily blood tests. They'd already packed up and left Folly Beach.

I called Greig and learned he'd started working a few hours each day. Also, he'd begun working through the list of home projects he'd generated while resting in his hospital bed.

Dr. Stuart remained satisfied with the results of his weekly blood tests and each time reduced more of his medication.

Eventually Greig's new immune system became 100 percent operational. His beautiful silver hair continued to grow. One day he realized it had returned curly.

God had followed him throughout many difficult years, had brought Glenn and others into his life to plant and water spiritual seeds, and had sealed his eternal destiny when he accepted Christ. God redeemed his life, shoving the old, sad, depressing days behind him and ushering him into the freedom to become the person God created him to be. I felt privileged to be able to observe the way God had worked in his life.

I asked my friends to keep praying for protection from germs, for a steady renewal of energy, and for his new immune system to hold any remaining leukemia cells in remission. The doctors planned to monitor him for at least a year but expected he would continue to recover well.

All of us praised God for this miracle of new life.

NOSTALGIC VISIT

Three months later Greig and I planned what we called my nostalgic visit. Driving north on the familiar freeway, I sang along with Christian songs floating from my CDs.

He and I viewed our reunion as a celebration of an amazing milestone in his journey toward restored health. The bone marrow transplant succeeded in keeping the leukemia cells in remission. Greig amazed everyone by the way he regained his strength and gradually started working again.

As I drove into his driveway, I saw him riding his backhoe near his garage. Dropping my bags in the house, I climbed down the back stairs.

"Hi Greig."

"Hey, hi. How are you?"

"Great. What are you up to?"

"Miguel is helping me with these leaves. I'm ready to take the next load to the back lot. Want to ride along?"

He reached out his hand to help me hop up on the huge yellow backhoe I'd seen in pictures he'd sent me from construction sites.

As we bounced along he explained, "I cleared out this entire back portion and divided it into two lots. That well serves both lots." His commentary made me feel like the master of an estate was giving me a guided tour.

While planning our reunion, I'd suggested the two of us stay overnight at Folly Beach for memory sake.

"I understand your idea, but for me it's in the past," he said. "I don't feel a need to go there again. But I'd like to pay for you to stay overnight at the Holiday Inn if you want to."

"Thanks, Greig. That's so thoughtful. I'll see if they'll give me a special rate."

During his recuperation at the Folly Beach condo, I'd walk the short distance to the beachfront Holiday Inn to jump online and check my emails. My daily appearances paved the way for friendships with the hotel personnel. They'd become aware of Greig's illness and transplant and stayed interested in his recovery.

Jay, the bell captain, often asked, "Gail, how is your brother? If there's anything you need, let me know."

Now I called the hotel and explained my situation. They wanted to give me a 50 percent discount so I agreed to let Greig treat me. I made a reservation and drove up on Saturday.

My room overlooked the beautiful ocean and pier. Quickly depositing my things, I hurried down the stairs to the same beach where Greig and I had walked during that uncertain time in our lives. I pictured him strolling with Harley in the early mornings.

Thank you, God, for the gift of Greig's transplant and his amazing recovery. You've given us hope for a full life for him.

That hotel stay completed a significant circle in my life.

Sunday afternoon I returned to Greig's house. Later Buster

walked in the back door to spend time with Greig during his three-day break from work. He hadn't seen his dad for a month.

Buster chuckled as he walked over to hug him. "You sure have lots of curls, don't you, Dad?"

Greig tried to catch up with some of the work he'd had to lay aside during his illness. At the end of Monday, Greig walked into the kitchen and plopped down at the table.

"I'm so tired."

"I'm not surprised. You were up on ladders and roofs all last week and today you did power washing."

Later that night, Casey called.

"Hey, Dad, you know that medallion I've been trying to finish for one of my flooring projects?"

"Yeah."

"Well, I'm having trouble with the circular cutter. Can you help me?"

"Sure, bring it over."

I knew Greig felt exhausted, but his desire to help his son won out.

Weekly Appointment

The next morning I rode with Greig for his weekly blood work and doctor appointment in Charleston. After the routine lab test, we moved to our assigned room to wait for Dr. Stuart's report.

I remembered other appointments during his recovery at the beach. One time when Dr. Stuart entered the room a smile spread across his face.

"You're looking good. You make us look good."

His comment encouraged me, but Greig never allowed himself to think he was home free.

He'd told me, "I've heard too many stories from nurses. Once patients gain their strength after a transplant, they'd often return to visit the nurses and talk about their future. But, before too long, the nurses learned they died."

Surely Dr. Stuart will have another good report today. I smiled as he and his assistant came in.

Dr. Stuart sat by Greig. "Your platelets are low this time, which sometimes happens if they clump together. We want to take another blood sample while you're here so we can retest it. Call me at home tonight and I'll let you know the result."

That evening we sat together at dinner, visiting as best we could with the unknown weighing on our minds. Finally Greig picked up the phone.

"Hello, Dr. Stuart. This is Greig."

He went silent, eyes staring at the floor. I knew. When he got off the phone he slowly stood up from his chair and leaned against the kitchen counter.

"I've had a relapse. He wants to see me tomorrow."

Speechless, I stood up and walked over to hug him.

The next morning, we headed back to Charleston. Absorbed in our own thoughts, we made the trip in silence.

Dr. Stuart came in and said, "Greig, I'm sorry that the tests confirmed you've had a relapse. Unfortunately, a relapse only three months after a transplant greatly reduces the odds of survival." His assistant looked at me with compassion.

"The next thing we can do," he said, "is infuse your body with some more cells from your donor. This will serve as a booster shot. My office will call to set your admittance date."

I had to leave the next day. Fortunately, with Buster home, Greig wouldn't be alone. Greig and I hugged each other several times while standing on his porch. Reluctantly I climbed into my car and waved goodbye.

We both anticipated a call on Monday. Instead, a nurse called on Friday. "Dr. Stuart needs to readmit you today. Come to his office first."

Greig called me at the office to let me know. "So soon? I would have tried to stay."

"That's OK. Buster will drive me."

Dr. Stuart explained to Greig and Buster, "You'd had an early relapse, but hope is still at a high level if you can fight successfully against graft vs. host during the first month. That term means the new immune system will view the body as foreign and continually attack it for a while. We need to give you some chemo before we give you additional donor cells."

Unexpected Battle

Only three months after we'd left Folly Beach with hope in our hearts for a healthy future, Greig entered the hospital again.

Immediately they began chemo.

Greig's new immune system gradually reduced the percentage of leukemia cells. However, it relentlessly attacked his digestive system. The results kept him bedridden.

Since I planned to return to Charleston, I called Tommy, the owner of the condo, to ask the cost of renting the condo again. "Well, instead of the spring rate, I'm going to give you the winter rate you had last time. I care about Greig and I hope he gets well."

At the condo I sat on the balcony looking out at the familiar beach. Tourists crowded onto the pier and the sand was now dotted with beach umbrellas, playful children, and boisterous teenagers on spring break. But spring hadn't arrived for me; it was still winter in my world.

Greig no longer waited for a bone marrow transplant or anticipated his release date so he could begin his recovery. This time he had been hospitalized because the transplant hadn't gone the way everyone had hoped. He had entered a more tenuous stage of his journey.

God, help me be strong. Help me not lose hope but continue believing you for Greig's recovery.

God brought to my mind His promise in Psalm 16:8. "I've set the Lord continually before me; because He is at my right hand, I will not be shaken."

Without Greig at the condo, adorable Harley became my companion. After our morning walk on the beach or along the boardwalk I'd load Harley in my car and make my way to the high-rise parking garage. I'd leave him some drinking water, open the window for a bit of fresh air and head to Greig's room.

Partway through the day I'd dash down to the car and take Harley for a quick walk. After a few more hours with Greig, Harley and I returned to our beach retreat.

Greig slept for long periods of time. Always glad for whatever rest he could get, I'd perch on the window bench and read a book. Whenever he opened his eyes, he'd look over to find me. Sometimes I felt inadequate to encourage him, but in those moments I hoped being there with him met his deepest need.

On Easter morning I decided to walk on the beach and talk with God before going to the hospital. So much had happened during the previous seven months that I needed extra time for refreshment and recharging.

After my walk I sat on the balcony, my feet propped up on the railing. I reflected on several verses that reminded me of God's perspective and His promises. "For momentary, light affliction is producing for us an eternal weight of glory far beyond all comparison, while we look not at the things which are seen but at the things which are not seen; for the things which are seen are temporal, but the things which are not seen are eternal."[1]

"We know that if the earthly tent which is our house is torn down, we have a building from God, a house not made with hands, eternal in the heavens."[2]

"Jesus said to her, 'I am the resurrection and the life. The one who believes in me will live, even though they die; and whoever lives by believing in me will never die. Do you believe this?"[3]

Father, thank you for Your assurance. I praise you that no matter what happens to Greig here on earth, he will never die. This is Resurrection Day. You didn't stay in the grave; You are alive. Because you overcame death, we will never die but will live with You forever. Thank you that both of us have Your promise of eternal life."

I longed for God to restore Greig's weakened body and grant him more years of life on earth. I didn't ask to know His plan; I chose to rest in His presence, cherishing that moment.

Later when I entered Greig's room, I found him sitting in a chair by the window dressed in khaki shorts, a green polo shirt that complemented his green eyes, and his comfortable white tennis shoes. We smiled at each other. I welcomed his obvious invitation to talk and sat in the chair next to him.

I don't recall our conversation that morning, but I will always remember that moment, sitting side by side as brother and sister. New hope embraced us like the bright morning sun rising from behind a silhouetted mountain peak.

I noticed Greig begin to shiver. Thinking he'd simply gotten chilled since he wasn't under the covers, I grabbed an extra blanket and threw it around his shoulders. We talked a while longer, but he didn't seem to warm up.

"Greig, why don't you try to get some sleep?"

"I feel really awful," he said as he climbed back into bed.

When he awoke, I walked over to his bed. Shocked when I saw his bright red face, I punched the call button. The nurse took his temperature and realized he had a significant fever.

Grateful I'd left Harley at the condo since I hadn't left there until after lunch, I sat back down to keep vigilance. As the hours passed, Greig slept fitfully. The nurses kept icing him.

Finally at 11 p.m., when the nurse took his temperature, it had lowered a bit. I asked her advice about driving home for a short night's rest. "That should be fine," she said.

Early the next morning I returned to the hospital. Hopeful that his fever had broken in the night, I stepped into his room. When I saw a washcloth curved across his forehead, his reddened face contorted with obvious discomfort, I knew the battle still raged. His fever had escalated, even though the nurses had kept him packed with ice throughout the night. I wished they'd called me.

Soon Dr. Stuart and his entourage walked into the room for their morning rounds.

Walking over to Dr. Stuart I asked, "His condition seems so serious. Shall I call his children?"

"No, not yet," he replied. "I think his fever will break. Let's give it some more time."

When they left I walked to his bedside, put my hand on his shoulder, and leaned over. "Greig, I'm here."

Returning to the window bench I prayed he could survive this crisis. Early afternoon a nurse took another reading. Beaming, she turned to me, "It's normal."

My heart soared as I praised God for hearing my prayer. I walked over to where he slept. A peaceful, relaxed expression replaced the discomfort I'd observed earlier. His normal coloring had returned.

When he awakened I said, "Greig, I'm so relieved your fever finally broke. How are you feeling now?"

Looking up at me with sober eyes he explained, "I was at death's door. I was very, very ill."

My arms rested lightly on his raised knees. "Well, it seems like God decided, 'You don't need to go through this door. You can go through this door,'" I said as I gestured from one side of his bony knees to the other.

Looking at me intently, he seemed to draw encouragement from the explanation and smiled slightly.

For the rest of my life I will regret not asking him to tell me more. I will never know what he really experienced until I have a chance to ask him in heaven. All I know is he stood at death's door but God broke his raging fever and spared his life. His time hadn't come yet.

He slept peacefully that night. Soon his body began producing white cells again. He smiled when he heard the news. Our hope rose again.

Richard's Shift

Richard returned to Folly Beach for several more weeks. He planned to visit Greig each day and take him back to the condo after his release.

He emailed me, "I was astounded when the doctor told me

two days after you left that he could leave the hospital. He looked so weak. But the doctor said his numbers were good and proceeded with the paperwork to release him."

After the almost unbearable strain of climbing six flights of stairs to the beach condo, Greig flopped on the coach. He remained there throughout each day and evening except for frequent trips to the bathroom. His immune system's attack on his digestive track continued to beat his weakened body. Despite daily visits to the hospital and frequent blood transfusions, Greig continued to decline. Finally, Doctor Stuart re-admitted him.

"Visiting Greig every day and always hearing the doctors say, 'Things are looking better, but it's not yet time for Greig to be released' frustrated me," Richard confided.

I returned to Charleston the day before Richard's departure. We walked into Greig's room together, Richard began his usual banter and they both laughed. It gave me a glimpse of the kind of time they had enjoyed during the previous weeks.

Richard and Greig's friendship had endured all odds. Now Greig faced a life-threatening illness. He needed Richard's support and Richard had come.

I pulled my camera out of my purse and asked, "Hey Greig, would you be willing for me to take a few pictures?"

Surprising me, he threw off the covers and climbed out of bed. He smiled as he posed with Richard and then with me. Only when looking at those pictures of Greig did I fully grasp how thin and gaunt he'd become.

As Richard left the next morning, we hugged each other. We'd become personal friends and mutual supporters, bound by shared experiences. I cried as I watched his car pull out of the carport. I felt alone. Harley plopped down in the carport, his head resting on his paws. Loneliness engulfed both of us like fog rising from the beach behind us.

My heart turned to Greig. Harley and I climbed the condo stairs to get ready for our visit to the hospital.

"You're here early," Greig said as I entered his room.

Not wanting to reveal my sadness or my eagerness to see him, I cited Richard's early departure as my reason for being there sooner than usual.

As the days passed, I settled into the routine of listening to the daily report from his doctor, helping Greig to and from the bathroom, enticing him to eat, and talking a little in between his naps. This time, though, my main concentration became my work responsibilities.

Looking back on that time, I wondered if my focus on work rather than my usual personal attentiveness to Greig stemmed from a feeling of inadequacy or incompetence in dealing with his fragile health. Or had I unconsciously given up after hearing the same doctor report day after day? Did my indifference camouflage deep emotions I didn't want to face? Had my weariness made me unable to think of ways to open conversations that might allow him to express his own feelings or fears?

As I pondered those questions, a deep sense of regret washed over me. I kept condemning myself, wishing I could change the way I had behaved and fearing it had disappointed Greig. After many confessions and conversations with God, I finally accepted the truth that God would never condemn me.[4] He confirmed that I had walked by faith and relied on Him.

I surrendered my self-accusations and accepted God's unconditional love for me, dispelling the schemes of the enemy who always seeks to discourage and defeat us. I thanked God for allowing me to spend time with Greig. God helped me realize that the only gift He wanted me to give Greig was simply to "be there" with him.

I continued my routine: visiting Greig each day at the hospital and communicating regularly with Richard. To his email inquiries, "How's it going there?" my weary reply remained the same: "Greig's so weak."

Richard had told me, "I left town feeling like Greig's 'road to recovery' stretched farther ahead than I'd originally anticipated, but still believing Greig would eventually be going home fully cured."

We both hung on to hope, but this time by a fraying rope. The doctors continued assuring me, "We are still aiming to get Greig strong enough to leave the hospital." It puzzled me because I saw no change. His new immune system continued to attack his body.

Greig didn't complain. He held on with amazing patience and calmness, hoping that one day he would turn the corner.

Several days before I left again, I called Carol. "I know you dislike driving long distances, but could you meet me at the hospital on Saturday and take Harley home with you? Maybe you could visit with Greig in the morning while I pack my things from the condo. Then I'll bring Harley to the hospital for you."

"Sounds like a plan." she said, "It'll be good to see Greig. It's been quite a while since he's been able to talk with me by phone. I'll call you when I'm finished there."

At the scheduled time, I packed the car and drove to the hospital parking lot to meet Carol. I got out of the car and hugged her, than noticed the joy beaming from her face.

"Greig and I had a good visit. He even said 'I love you' when I left. You know, that was a difficult thing for him to say before we divorced. Afterwards, I still kept saying 'I love you' even if he didn't say anything in return."

That afternoon she had heard those longed-for words. Perhaps Greig knew it would be his last time to tell her. Though divorced, they never lost their love for each other.

After hugging Harley, my sweet companion, I handed him to Carol. I watched them leave and then hustled up to Greig's room for a quick goodbye.

"I wish I didn't have to leave town."

"I understand. It was nice to see Carol but I'm really tired now anyway. Thanks for all you're doing for me."

I gave him a quick hug, smiled at him and promised to keep in touch. I held my tears until I reached the elevator, grateful to have it to myself for the ride to the first floor.

Once on the road for my seven-hour drive, my emotions flowed freely.

Lord, it's so hard to see him weak and suffering. Every day we keep hoping the battle will be over and he can begin to recover again. You provided a perfect match for the transplant. He did so well for three months. Why did things have to change, Lord?

I sensed no answer.

More Father-Daughter Time

After Regan arrived several days later, she left her dad's bedside only for quick bites to eat. She had brought love and light into Greig's life from the first day they met. Now her presence in those days of silent despair lifted Greig's spirits.

The doctors tried everything they could to reverse the downward spiral. Greig continued to fight with courage but as the days passed, Regan began to struggle in the same way Richard and I had. She heard the same words from the doctor every day and witnessed Greig's weakening condition, causing her to wonder if her dad would survive.

One Saturday morning, Regan called me.

"Aunt Gail, Dad's taken a turn for the worse. Can you come?"

"I'll be there as soon as I pack the car."

Regan and I agreed to meet at a nearby Wendy's for dinner. Across the table she explained, "When I walked into his room this morning, I saw a nurse standing by his bed. She told me that Friday night after I had returned to the condo, Dad fell in the bathroom. His vital organs began to fluctuate and now he is in a coma. They called Casey not me. I didn't want to leave his bedside to get something to eat and now I'm famished. So glad you could come, Aunt Gail."

After a quick hamburger we returned to the hospital. Bracing ourselves for the worst, we walked through the familiar corridors to Greig's room.

As I drew near to Greig's bedside I gazed at his silent face.

Regan lovingly rubbed his bald head and said, "Hi, Dad. Gail is here."

Suddenly he moved and struggled to open his eyes as if to see me. Regan and I looked at each other with surprise.

"He knows I'm here," I shouted. My heart leaped. I praised God for this gift to me.

Regan and I stayed at his bedside throughout each day. Talking, crying and remembering.

Casey came to Folly Beach the last two days of his dad's life, sometimes sitting alone with him. Grateful for the time he'd had to say parting words to his dad, I hoped that this experience would fortify him for the future storms of life.

During his entire illness, Greig dealt with his circumstances calmly. He never resigned; instead, he chose to accept his condition. He kept fighting and saying yes to the next step, whatever the odds. None of us heard him complain. Courage remained his trademark, drawing the admiration of his family and all the medical personnel.

With heavy hearts we knew the time had come to choose a crematorium. We decided on a place near Greig's home, and drove to meet Edith Galloway, the director of the funeral home.

We had asked God to numb our hearts enough to handle the details. As soon as Edith walked into the waiting area and said, "I am here to help you," we felt at peace. In those difficult moments, she became like an older sister, guiding us as we made crucial decisions.

The next day, June 21, we sat at Greig's bedside talking with each other and whispering words of love and thanks to him as he quietly breathed, his eyes shut.

As we left his room that evening, we silently rode the elevator to the first floor. As the doors opened, there stood Dr. Stuart. Emotions collided in my heart—appreciation, desperation, disappointment.

As tears ran down my face I choked out, "Thank you for all you did to try to save Greig's life."

Despite my mixed emotions, I was grateful to see Dr. Stuart face to face one more time. I knew I would never need to talk to him again. Greig was taking his final steps toward heaven and away from Regan and me.

Home at Last

That night the hospital called. After listening to the official words, I knocked on Regan's bedroom door and tiptoed into her room. Startled, she turned toward me.

"Regan, I'm so sorry to have to tell you your dad is gone."

Embracing each other, we cried softly. Regan said, "Dad told me, 'I'm ready for this to end, one way or the other.'"

After calling the others, we somehow managed to sleep until early morning. Throwing on my bathrobe I shuffled into the front room. A little note propped against a loaf of banana bread caught my attention.

Aunt Gail, I'm walking on the beach for a little while. I'll be back soon. Regan xoxo.

Our shared experience bound us together forever. Gratitude filled our hearts for not having to face those last days alone.

Later we walked on the beach together. Seeing the waves flop onto the shore, hearing the cries of sea gulls mixed with the giggles of children, smelling the salt air, watching families wander down the wooden pier somehow breathed hope into us for the future. A life had been snuffed out, but our lives would continue. More difficult experiences would splash into our lives, but joy would rise up in the morning.

"I want to gather some sand where I know dad walked," Regan said as she bent down to lift some sand into her zip lock bag.

I lifted handfuls of sand into the bag she had brought for me.

"Aunt Gail, what are you going to do with all that sand?"

"Not sure," I replied sheepishly.

We wandered into the beach gift shop. Enjoying the diversion, we laughed over the odd collection of shell gifts. Browsing through the T-shirts, I chose a deep pink one with "Experience Folly Beach" stretched across the front. Greig liked pink on me. A small glass with a blue sand dollar painted above a "Folly Beach" engraving caught my eye.

A sense of relief replaced the pressure we had felt during many months of wondering, waiting, praying, hoping. We felt recharged for what lay ahead.

Remembering Greig

Before we left town, I drove alone to the hospital to collect Greig's personal belongings. For the first time, the elevator would not take me to see Greig. My only purpose in being there would be to thank those who had helped me throughout his long journey and to pick up clothes he no longer needed.

Turning the corner of the cancer unit, I approached the nurse's station.

"Hi, Stephanie."

"I'm so sorry about your brother, Gail. Two nurses who came on duty on Wednesday sobbed in the hallway when they heard the news. They really liked him."

Struggling to hold back my tears, I said, "Thanks for telling me. And thanks for all the times you listened to me and assured me of your prayers. You helped me a lot."

"You're welcome. I know this is a hard time for you."

Next I went to find his nurse, who was a Christian sister. "Jill, I wanted to thank you for your advice and encouragement about Greig's condition. And thanks for the chance to talk about spiritual things, too. You were God's gift to me." She reached out and hugged me.

One of the other nurses led me to the storage room to retrieve Greig's bag. As I started back down the hallway I froze. Fresh sheets covered the empty bed where he'd spent the last three months of his courageous journey. With a broken heart, I walked on toward the next chapter of my own journey.

On the chosen day our family and Greig's close friends gathered around the beautiful oak tree in his yard to celebrate his life. Regan facilitated our gathering, which included a chance to share stories and remembrances of Greig. Richard's wife, Sandy, read our short tribute from the memorial folder.

Though his life was too short, Greig lived life to the fullest!

His adventurous spirit captivated us all.

He showed kindness and generosity toward family and close friends.

He could always find a solution for any problem.

He never did anything half-heartedly.

He took pride in all aspects of his life.

He loved us all.

Though he will be missed, he would not want us to be sad. His spirit will always be alive in each and every one of us.

He loved us, touched our lives and taught us so much, and he would want us to continue to embrace life and live it to the fullest as he would.

I looked around the circle at the brave faces of Regan, Jake, Casey and Buster.

Regan and Greig's relationship as father and daughter spanned a shorter amount of time than it would have if circumstances had been different. She told me while we were together in Folly Beach, "I don't regret the lost years with dad. We had more than twenty years together to build memories I can hold onto forever."

Jake launched out on his own at eighteen, securing a job in Montana. As Jake reached adulthood, he and his dad reconnected. I remembered the pleasure on Greig's face whenever Jake called his hospital room. He became an encourager to his dad and always thanked me for taking care of him.

Always on the go, Casey hadn't had time for father-son chats in the early years. After starting his own flooring business, Casey relished his dad's advice on solving design problems. He related to the small group gathered around the oak tree, "Dad always knew how to do everything. I will miss calling him up for advice."

Buster wore no particular expression as we stood together. Yet I knew he would miss his dad the most. After graduating, he continued living with Greig and helping him with his business before entering his own career. Buster had said, "I said to Dad one time, 'You have taken me so many places, taught me so many things, and helped me experience so many adventures that if I died today I'd be a happy man.' I'm so glad I told him that."

Now all together for his memorial service, we took turns spreading some of Greig's ashes at the base of the tree on the property he loved.

Once the group moved inside the house for refreshments and visiting, I talked with Tony, Greig's young friend from work who had joined us.

"Greig was always very kind to me," he told me. "He taught me about building, but he also listened to my personal stories. Life hasn't always been easy for me, but I feel like Greig cared about me. I wanted to come here today because of what he did for me. I will miss him."

After the friends had left, I remembered a picture I'd taken at Greig's place on my way to the Charleston hospital. Pulling my computer out, I called to the others and they gathered around me.

As the picture came up, Jake gasped. "Aunt Gail, that's awesome."

"Can't believe the way the sun is shining through the branches," Regan said. "Let's call it our memorial tree."

"You all want a copy?"

"Yes," they said in unison.

God had created that picture of the majestic oak tree to give us something we could all treasure. I had no inkling we would spread Greig's ashes at its base less than a year later.

After a couple more days together, Jake and Regan flew back to their homes. Casey and Jessica went about their life in town. Buster stepped up into his long, white, 18-wheeler for his next month-long road trip.

We were sad to say goodbye, but we were connected now. Our new relationships would provide comfort and strength during the great adjustment in our lives.

Handling Estate Affairs

As personal representative for Greig's estate, I stayed at the house a few more days to make phone calls, close out credit cards, and establish an estate bank account. Greig's orderly filing system enabled me to find everything I needed.

I had called the rental office to verify where to mail the check to cover the remaining weeks of the contract for the Folly Beach condo. They said they'd call me back after talking with Tommy.

The next day the office relayed the answer. "Tommy said to tell you everything is taken care of and he is sorry for your loss." I cried.

Tommy's kindness reminded me, once again, that I had nothing to fear. God would take care of every detail, as He promised in Isaiah 41:10. "Do not fear, for I am with you; do not anxiously look about you, for I am your God. I will strengthen you, surely I will help you, surely I will uphold you with My righteous right hand."

On my last day, after washing my breakfast dishes, drying the last load of clothes, and handling a few details with our lawyer Alisa, I backed my car out of Greig's driveway. Then reality hit me. I'd be back in town to visit my nephews and handle additional estate affairs, but Greig would never be there to greet me. Ever.

Walking into the Future

Greig and I were both wayward children. We searched for love and approval in different ways. Greig's search ended when he stepped into heaven. Wrapped in the arms of His God, he finally heard, "I always loved and accepted you. Welcome home, son!"

Meanwhile, here on earth, I clung to God's promise that He loves and accepts me as I am. He declares, "You are the apple of my eye."[5] He sings songs of love over me.[6] I no longer need to strive for His love. Nothing will cause Him to love me more than He does already. Nothing I ever do will disgust Him, displease Him or cause Him to withdraw His love from me or turn away. He wraps His arms around me[7] and He will always shelter me under His wings during all storms of life.[8]

Each day takes me closer to heaven. One day I'll see my childhood friend, my brave and caring brother, and wrap my arms around him. Together, we will be enveloped in God's unending world of love and acceptance.

MOTHER OF THE GROOM

Sitting on my own couch again, I gazed at the array of pictures parading across my coffee table. All four pictures now represented loved ones who were no longer here.

I cried out, "Greig, I didn't want you to go. I didn't think you would leave me so soon."

Grief, suppressed since my first visit to see him at the Savannah hospital, erupted in an avalanche of uncontrollable sobs. *My family is gone. I am alone.*

Each one left an empty spot, but losing Greig so early caused my heart's deepest pain. We were peers. We should have had more visits, more catch-up calls, more cheery happy birthday wishes, and more hugs.

Whenever alone at home, I couldn't control my tears. My heart was broken. I feared it always would be.

To try to get a grip on my emotions, I searched for comfort in my daily routine. Working in the office, being with friends, and attending fun activities helped soften the loneliness. I began focusing on a happy event on my calendar, a trip to Portland to see Aunt Elia and the family.

My visits had become less frequent since Mom died. Yet I'd always been grateful for Aunt's Elia's support during Mom's untimely hospitalization and death. Mom's absence had left a hole in my heart, but I tried to encourage Aunt Elia in her own adjustment of losing her only sibling.

Now I wanted to help her celebrate the upcoming wedding of her older son Blair. At least I'd have two months to continue adjusting to the loss of Greig before making my trip.

I sent a brief email to Blair. "Hey, how's it going? What's happening with you? Look forward to seeing you when I come in September."

I intended to catch a glimpse of his daily life to help me more easily jump into the flow of the family once I arrived. His response startled me. It centered on only one thing.

"Mom hasn't been feeling well."

Aunt Elia? She's been healthy all her life. What could be wrong?

Eventually her doctor concluded that her rapid gain of fluid and shortness of breath indicated congestive heart failure.

A subsequent email took a more serious turn. "Mom isn't improving. Please pray."

Lord, this can't be happening. I've said goodbye to Mom, Dad, Addi and Greig. I need Aunt Elia in my life. Please protect her.

When Aunt Elia had received the news of my birth, she wrote my mother from college. "I can't wait to meet Gail when I come home on spring break."

As a young girl I looked up to my sophisticated aunt. She intrigued me with her pretty dresses, interesting hats, and high heels. As a buyer at Olds & Kings department store, she traveled frequently in the Northwest. She occasionally babysat Greig and me.

She'd majored in Home Economics and sewed beautifully. Proudly I presented to her everything I stitched in my 7th and 8th grade Home Economics classes.

When she got engaged at thirty-three, the exciting news coursed through our family circuit. To celebrate, Mom planned an afternoon picnic. All of us gathered around the wooden picnic table in the corner of our long, grassy backyard.

I felt special when Aunt Elia chose me to handle her wedding book. Mother and I shopped for my dress at "her" store. We both liked the light-blue polished cotton dress, but before making a purchase Mom felt compelled to walk to Aunt Elia's department to solicit her approval. Her smile gave us the green light.

The wedding created wonderful memories for all of us. Afterwards Aunt Elia and Uncle Miles moved to Hawaii since my uncle had accepted a two-year assignment in connection with his work. They stayed in communication with Mark, Pamela and Lynn, my uncle's three children from a previous marriage.

Blair was born in Hawaii. Seven years later, Aunt Elia gave birth to their son Cary.

Everyone congregated at their home for holidays because of the large dining area and the lovely pool framed by plenty of lawn. Uncle Miles grilled or cooked the meat, while the women prepared the rest of the food. Aunt Elia always made the same request of Mom, "Marjorie, can you bring your pies?" Depending on the weather, everyone swam in the pool after the meal.

A Different Home

Mom's unexpected death devastated everyone, especially Aunt Elia. She was eleven years younger than Mom, so they'd not been close growing up. Later in life they'd become best friends.

In the midst of her sadness Aunt Elia said, "Gail, I want you to be part of our family now and stay with us whenever you are in town. You will be like the daughter I never had."

I appreciated her kind words but wondered what those future visits would look like. I couldn't remember confiding in her about personal things as a mother and daughter might do. Because of her invitation, I stayed at their home during my furloughs from the Philippines, but we struggled in our relationship.

I prayed a lot, asking God to show me why she often criticized my words and actions. God helped me see that I'd placed unfair expectations on her by assuming my furlough times would be the same as they had been when I stayed with Mom.

The two sisters had different personalities and ways of relating to people. Aunt Elia didn't enjoy sitting down for lengthy conversations, meeting my friends, or being involved in my activities.

Mom and I had enjoyed talking and doing things together. We'd become a team of two and easily coordinated our schedules. Aunt Elia needed to give time and attention to Uncle Miles, be available to their grown children as needed, and spend time with the grandchildren. I shared Mom's phone and car; Aunt Elia and Uncle Miles couldn't offer those conveniences.

God helped me release my expectations and look for

opportunities to reciprocate for their help. He also showed me ways to communicate love to Aunt Elia since expressing love was not easy for her.

Each time I planned a furlough I'd email her ahead of time. "Aunt Elia, what do you want to do together while I'm home? I'll block those times out."

She began to soften, allowing me entrance into her life in a way she'd not done previously. We began looking forward to going to a movie, talking over lunch at a new restaurant, and attending cultural events. Gradually we built a loving and giving relationship.

Nothing to Offer

Because of all that had transpired to create our closeness, I struggled with the news of her illness. Was our relationship going to come to an end? New grief wrapped itself around the base of my exhausted heart like an unwanted weed.

Physically, mentally, and emotionally depleted, with unfinished grief over Greig's death, I prayed to God.

Lord, I have no energy left, nothing to offer her; but I must go.

Arriving in Portland, I drove my rented car through the familiar streets. I slipped into a visitor's parking slot, locked the car, and walked toward the five-story retirement center where my aunt and uncle lived. In the lobby, I signed in at the reception desk and headed toward the elevator.

Slowly the elevator ascended to the third floor. *Will she look pale and sickly? Is she going to die? What should I say to the family?*

My cousin Cary opened the door. Beyond him I saw my lovely aunt, sitting in a wheelchair and smiling at me. Her black skirt, silk blouse, and makeup camouflaged her illness. Only her bloated stomach signaled something out of the ordinary. I bent down to slip my arm around her shoulders and hugged her.

"Aunt Elia, I'm so glad to see you."

"Hi, honey. I'm happy you're here."

Blair stood by her side, ready to wheel her down to the dining room. As we visited around our table everything seemed normal.

After dinner I strolled alongside Aunt Elia's wheelchair back to their apartment. Hugging her goodbye, I headed to the home of Becky and Bill, long-time friends who lived ten minutes away.

"She looks good," I related to them as I walked into their home. "We'll be together for Sunday lunch tomorrow."

The next day on my way back to the retirement center after church, I noticed a voicemail and hit the button to listen.

"Gail, this is Cary. Dad had to take mom to the hospital early this morning. She was sick all night. She's at Milwaukie Providence Hospital."

I turned the car around and sped toward the hospital.

Warding off sad memories, I rushed to her room. As if on autopilot I sprang into action, adjusting her pillow and bending the straw for her to sip some water.

The following morning I found her sitting up in bed reading a magazine. "I feel so much better," she said. "They removed 4 ½ liters of liquid."

She continued, "I have to tell you a funny story. This morning a nurse began asking me questions from her medical history form. 'When was your last hospital stay?' she said. I told her, 'Forty-six years ago when I gave birth to my youngest son.' Her next question was, 'Do you smoke?' I answered, 'I haven't smoked for fifty-two years.'"

I laughed, grateful to see her smiling.

Her sickness puzzled all of us. Her former doctor had treated her for congestive heart failure, but she wasn't improving. Now Cary and Blair met with a different doctor at the hospital.

Cary pointed out, "The symptoms don't match up with congestive heart failure. We feel like something else is wrong."

"I agree," he said. "I plan to run additional tests."

Correct Diagnosis

Cary called me several days later. "The tests show Mom has ovarian cancer. No wonder she wasn't getting better with the previous treatment."

"Cary, I'm so sorry. How is your dad?"

"I think he's numb. But at least we know what's going on."

The doctor released Aunt Elia to the care center at their residence. Their friends could visit her whenever they wanted. Uncle Miles popped in twice a day, eventually requesting his dinners to be delivered to her room so they could eat together.

She set only one goal: be strong enough to walk down the aisle at Blair's wedding. By sheer determination she began physical therapy, taking tentative steps behind a walker.

I'd happily stepped into the role of personal assistant. Each day I breezed into her room, hugged her, and reached for my small pad to record more notes.

"Gail, next time you go to the apartment look for the birthday card on my desk," she instructed. "I need to mail it to Fran this week."

I also made a note to bring over the dress and jewelry she'd decided to wear for the wedding.

Her illness brought an end to her regular activities. But she accepted this inevitable change and remained cheerful as the days progressed. She simply checked things off her to-do list.

One day she announced, "Oh, I made some phone calls and sold our opera tickets." A lover of music and the arts, she couldn't bear for the remainder of her season tickets to go unused.

Mother of the Groom

She agreed to use a wheelchair at the wedding but remained intent on walking down the aisle. Her dress waited for her in the closet.

The wedding day arrived. I went to help Aunt Elia get ready. Too excited to wait for me, she had straightened her hair—styled the day before by the center's beautician—applied her makeup, and requested the nurse's help in putting on her attractive, colorful dress.

"You look beautiful," I exclaimed as I entered her room. I put on her earrings and necklace to complete her perfect look as mother of the groom.

Cary had ordered a limousine so we could more easily visit during the long ride to the wedding site. We had tried to keep this plan a secret. As the nurse brought in a wheelchair, she whispered to me, "I saw the limo out front and wondered if it was for her." I hoped Aunt Elia hadn't heard. If she did, she didn't say.

She lowered herself into the wheelchair. Once outside she saw the limo. I explained it was a gift from Cary and she smiled with delight.

The uniformed driver helped her into the back row. I sunk into one of the side seats. When Cary and his girlfriend Juli arrived, they claimed the front section of the wide circle of plush black leather seats.

Our limo driver chauffeured the four of us a short distance to the main entrance of the retirement center. Uncle Miles rose from the outside bench with a smile on his face. He looked suave and handsome in his black jacket, gray pants, and grey and black striped tie lying snuggly against his crisp white shirt.

The driver lowered Aunt Elia's side window and she smiled and waved to him. Once he crawled into the seat next to her, she quipped, "Well, we might as well hold hands."

As predicted, rain began falling during the two-hour trip. Blair and Peggy had planned for their marriage to take place on the lawn overlooking the beautiful vineyard with the reception in the heated tent afterwards.

The rain altered their plan. The clubhouse workers motioned

the group to move inside and find our assigned seats. They laid a makeshift dance floor on the grass in one corner of the tent and lowered the plastic windows. Artificial trees and soft lights created a wonderland. While rain beat on the plastic windows, we all sat comfortably as heaters blew warm air into the tent.

The bride and groom and wedding party approached the tent under umbrellas and marched toward the wooden floor where the pastor stood. My aunt and uncle sat close to the makeshift stage, grateful that she no longer had to walk down an aisle during the ceremony.

When the time came for picture taking, the photographer instructed the wedding party to take their places. Cary assumed he would push his mother in the wheelchair and Uncle Miles would follow. Instead, Aunt Elia insisted on walking.

Cary lifted her up and I reached for her arm to help her gain her balance. Aware of the pressure she exerted on me, I realized she would be thrown off balance if I let go. As if on cue, I walked by her side.

When we reached the wooden floor, I prepared to step aside so Uncle Miles could take his place beside her. Then she moaned, "Oh no." Fearing she would faint, I held on to her more securely and called to Cary to get her wheelchair.

"No, I don't want the wheelchair," she exclaimed.

"Cary, please bring it over and set it behind her."

Cary dashed for the wheelchair and returned to grab his mother's arm again. Holding her tight, we turned her around to face the photographer. Knowing if we let go she would collapse, we both stayed by her side. I wondered where my uncle was in the lineup, but I smiled at the camera, hoping I didn't look as scared as I felt.

As soon as the pictures were taken, she willingly lowered herself into her wheelchair behind her. I breathed a sigh of relief.

Aunt Elia looked radiant—more beautiful than I'd ever seen her. No one looking at the joy radiating from her face that day would have guessed she had a serious illness. I believe her illness enabled her to embrace God in a new way and become the woman He wanted her to be. The beauty and joy I saw in her would live in my heart and mind forever.

We stayed a while longer, especially to visit with family who had driven a long distance for the occasion. Eventually, with umbrellas angled to ward off the rain, we moved from the tent to the limo for our drive home. The ceremony and reception represented an amazing milestone for my aunt and created a lasting memory for all of us. My heart filled with love and admiration for her courage and desire to keep this a happy occasion for her son.

Back in town, Aunt Elia hugged her husband goodbye, we said goodbye to Cary and Juli, and I wheeled her inside. Carefully undressing her, I helped her into bed.

As she lay down she sighed, "This feels so good. Wasn't that a wonderful time?"

"Aunt Elia, you looked beautiful tonight." I leaned down to hug her.

She pulled me closer and said, "I never could have done this without you, honey. Thank you."

In that moment all the years of heartache and resentment melted away. Finally I knew she approved of me, and loved and accepted me. Healing and redemption had come.

I moved away from her bed, knowing she needed to sleep. Though exhausted, happiness still radiated from her face.

Pausing at the door I smiled. "See you at Thanksgiving, Aunt Elia."

"I'll look forward to that," she said, her eyes twinkling.

On my drive back to Becky's home, I asked God to strengthen her and give us more time.

End of a Journey

Soon after I left Portland, Aunt Elia's condition stabilized. The care center released her to return to the apartment. Uncle Miles was thrilled.

One evening I called. "Hi, Uncle Miles. Calling to find out how Aunt Elia is."

"She's right here with me on the couch," he said.

I pictured them together again, as if nothing had changed.

During another phone call, Aunt Elia said, "Oh, honey, wanted to tell you that I sold my car."

I admired the way she faced death with courage. Never moaning or complaining, she accepted her condition, continued to close out necessary details of her life, and trusted God with the days she had left.

"She's excited to see her parents and her sister," Uncle Miles told me.

I knew his heart wrestled with her excitement and his inevitable devastation.

I clung to my hope to see her at Thanksgiving. Early in October Cary emailed that his mom had been hospitalized due to digestive problems caused by her first chemo treatment.

The doctor began monitoring her again. Family members arranged to take Uncle Miles to visit her each day. He and I kept in touch regularly.

The chirp of my cell phone startled me awake in the early morning hours of October 18. I flew out of bed.

"Gail, I wanted to let you know that Elia died tonight."

"Oh, Uncle Miles. I'm so sorry. I know it's a blessing for her as she no longer needs to suffer. But how are you doing?"

"I spent the whole day with her at the hospital, holding her hand," he said. "We talked together and she told me, 'We've had a good life. Thank you.' When I left her in the early evening, I bent down and kissed her. She pulled me closer and hugged me. I think she knew."

Celebrating a Life

Details for her memorial service began to fall into place. Cary and Pamela discussed what to include in the obituary. I sent Cary a copy of the obituary I'd written for Dad.

"Thanks so much," Cary said. "I wouldn't have known how

to get started."

Helping each other. Mutual sharing.

The day of the service, the family gathered for a brunch at a restaurant overlooking the river. Many had traveled from other places, including my uncle's son Mark and daughter Lynn. I watched my uncle enjoying his children and grandchildren, though without his precious wife of fifty-two years by his side.

Once we arrived at the church, the family visited with one another in various places. However, my uncle happened to be in the narthex as people began to arrive. One by one people imparted words of consolation and explained how much Aunt Elia had meant to them. He smiled, drank in their words, and relaxed.

Aunt Elia's best friend Francis, who had driven from Washington with her daughter Sally, walked toward him. Aunt Elia and Francis grew up together, became sorority sisters at the same university, and stayed in close contact the rest of their lives. With lips quivering, Francis and Uncle Miles embraced each other with mutual sadness. Both had lost their best friend.

The conversations flowed right up until time for the service to begin. Uncle Miles, now more peaceful, walked with confidence to the front row.

Change of Heart

After the service, some of the family gathered in Uncle Mile's apartment. We shared memories, laughed about family experiences, and looked at photo albums. The memorial service now behind us, we relaxed and relished the chance to be together.

We came from various branches of the family with different experiences and challenges, but we became one family through our shared loss. God washed away family disappointments and disagreements of the past. A new day had dawned, a day that would mark the beginning of healing.

Lynn's husband and son had driven back to Washington, leaving her behind to stay with her dad for several days.

Pulling Pamela and me aside she confided, "I'm scared. I don't know what to do. I've never stayed here before and I don't know where things are or how to help dad."

Realizing her fear rested on much deeper things, Pamela put her arm around Lynn.

"You'll be fine. You'll know what to do." Pamela's assurance seemed to calm her.

As a stepdaughter, Lynn had seldom felt welcomed by Aunt Elia. She had also experienced distance in her relationship with her father because of unspoken hurts.

Once she and her dad were by themselves, they talked, cried, and connected. Lynn reminisced about their early days together before her parents divorced. Happy memories surfaced, shifting their perspective of the past. They enjoyed outings and meals together.

Through that first visit, they both experienced a change of heart. Aunt Elia's death caused Uncle Miles deep pain and sadness, but his loss paved the way for a new father-daughter relationship to emerge.

Before leaving the church, Cary had pulled me aside to say he wanted to stay in closer touch with me. After returning to my home, I popped off an email, thanking him for all he had done and assuring him I would stay in touch. I closed with, "Love, your cousin Gail." His immediate response drew my attention.

"Thanks for your email, Gail. But I want you to know you're more than my cousin. You were the daughter my mother never had. I will always love you as my sister."

I cried. I had suffered loss, but I had gained a closer relationship with Cary than I'd experienced before. He adored my mother and I loved his. We both lost our mothers, but we still had each other.

Uncle Miles and I began calling each other weekly, a highlight for both of us. At first we compared our grief. Eventually he began to report on his progress in adjusting to his loss. Soon current personal stories dominated our conversations.

On one of my visits while Aunt Elia was still alive I'd asked him, "Uncle Miles, why do you always introduce me as Aunt Elia's niece? I'm your niece, too, you know. I've always felt you were my real uncle. Mom always felt like you were her real brother."

Now that we've had a chance to build our own personal friendship, he says to people, "This is my niece."

SEE YOU IN HEAVEN

The loss of many loved ones had carved deep ravines in my heart where rivers of sorrow flowed. My uncle's weekly phone calls helped build bridges over the dark waters.

Carol also encouraged me. Her marriage to Greig had lasted seventeen years, ending in divorce mainly due to his inability to overcome his alcoholism. Though they had developed other relationships after that time, neither of them had remarried. Instead, they kept ending up in the same city, supposedly coincidentally. Carol prepared Greig's taxes; he often repaired things at her home. Greig had explained to me, "Carol and I are better friends not married."

Carol and I began building a new kind of relationship when Greig received his diagnosis. During his first hospitalization, Carol had relied on my progress reports since I visited him every day. We hadn't had a chance to see each other yet.

After a waiting period that stretched to fifty days, Greig finally received clearance to return home and wait for news of a possible bone marrow transplant. I drove up to South Carolina to help around the house and cook for him.

One day, while in the kitchen with Jessica, I heard a knock at the door. Jessica went to check and returned to the kitchen.

"It's Carol," she said.

When Carol walked into the kitchen a few minutes later I

didn't recognize her. More than twenty years had passed and she looked so different.

"Well, hi, Gail. Nice to see you again."

"Good to see you too, Carol." My heart fluttered with unexpected delight.

A Family Thanksgiving

When the days slid into the Thanksgiving season Greig announced to me, "I talked to Buster and Casey about being together for Thanksgiving. I invited Carol, too."

Thanksgiving used to be their favorite holiday. Carol always prepared a special meal, a change from their usual unstructured meal times. As far as I knew, the family hadn't celebrated that holiday together since the divorce.

The date for our celebration hinged on Buster's break from his on-the-road work. When he received confirmation he would be back in town on Saturday, we set Sunday noon for our meal. Carol and I began phoning each other about food assignments.

"I'll make an apple pie and bring the vegetables and rolls," Carol related with excitement.

Greig got a good deal on a turkey and I bought ingredients for the dressing, mashed potatoes and gravy.

I relished the victory of finding inexpensive serving platters, matching plates, cups and bowls, eating utensils, and coordinated placemats and napkins. As two bachelors, Greig and Buster contentedly survived with mostly plastic plates and utensils. The house needed a woman's touch.

"Oh, that's a nice touch," he'd say each time I brought home another purchase.

While surveying his kitchen I mentioned to Greig, "Looks like I'll need a deeper pot to cook the potatoes."

By the end of the day a large Teflon pot appeared on the counter. I smiled at Greig's engagement in the details of this important occasion.

Sunday finally arrived and preparations spun into full operation. I cleared the long table in the front room, replacing the clutter of papers, files folders, and mail with the assortment of serving dishes and table settings I had acquired.

Soon wonderful aromas permeated the entire house. The smell of turkey, placed in the oven hours before, enticed our taste buds. When Carol arrived with her pie the scent of cinnamon and butter floating over softened apples made us long for a sample.

Buster sauntered in from his room about the time Casey, Jessica, and their three-year-old daughter Piper arrived. Meanwhile Carol and I worked side by side to put finishing touches on the rest of our meal while Greig sliced the turkey.

When we'd settled at the table, I offered to say a blessing. As I thanked God that our family could be together, I choked up.

I lifted my eyes and looked around at the seven of us. Greig's chemo had robbed him of his beautiful gray hair, but his baldness meant nothing to him or to us that day. He was alive. And we were together for Thanksgiving.

We finally pushed away from the table, stomachs full and satisfied. Carol, Greig and I began clearing the table and loading the dishwasher. After we finished the cleanup, Greig and I were left in the kitchen by ourselves. We smiled at each other. I opened my arms. Not a demonstrative person, he hesitated.

When I said, "Happy Thanksgiving," he realized the reason for my gesture and put his arms around me.

We'd been together as a family for the special holiday, enjoying a wonderful meal and happy chatter. But more than that, the two of us knew we had helped create a lasting family memory no one could take away from us in spite of what may lay ahead.

As usual, I documented the day in pictures. My favorite shows Greig, Carol, Casey and Buster, hugging each other with beaming smiles and the light gleaming off Greig's shiny bald head.

Soon Greig disappeared into his garage. Not long afterwards he walked into the house and announced to Carol, "I finished sanding the bench you brought over."

We all walked outside to see his handiwork.

"Oh, I knew you would get the wood grain to show the way I wanted," Carol exclaimed. "Thank you."

He carried the bench to her truck and turned to her. "Thanks for coming." She smiled as they hugged briefly.

Their gestures confirmed the love and friendship they both still enjoyed. Tears of joy threatened to overflow as I realized the importance of the two of them being together that day, in light of Greig's tentative health situation.

Carol and I continued communicating while I helped in Charleston during Greig's recovery from his bone marrow transplant. Whenever too much time lapsed I'd receive a call.

"Hi Gail. I'm worried. Haven't heard from Greig or you. He used to call me. What is happening?"

I didn't see Carol again until June when I turned Harley over to her at the hospital. Neither of us dreamed Greig's life would end less than three weeks later.

After his death, Carol and I continued our friendship. She supplied comfort, moral support, and advice in my unwelcomed role as personal representative of Greig's estate.

She also stepped up to fill some of the gaps left in her son's lives in the absence of their father. Together we all built a new kind of family, a family with different personalities, perspectives and experiences but shared memories that would link us forever.

Buster's News

The following year, in the middle of March, Buster called me. We liked talking to each other, but usually I initiated the calls.

Our conversation began with normal banter. Then his voice changed.

"One of the reasons I'm calling is to ask if you could advance me some money."

He never asked for money.

"Mom has been diagnosed with pancreatic cancer. She hadn't been feeling well. I told her she should see a doctor. We never expected this."

God, this can't be happening. The boys lost their dad less than a year ago. Now will they lose their mother, too?

The next time Buster called he told me the doctors had given his mom three months or less. I wondered where her heart stood with God. Years ago during a visit with the family I'd shared with her about God's love and His offer of eternal life.

"Well, I really can't make that decision if Greig doesn't. That won't work," she'd said.

I couldn't dispute her thinking. Greig showed no interest in spiritual things. Still, disappointment rose in my heart.

After Carol's diagnosis, we talked a few times by phone. She seemed more willing to listen when the topic of God came up. Still she expressed no interest in considering His offer.

After a first round of chemo administered in the hospital, her condition stabilized. Buster took her to Greig's home, which he'd been renting since his dad's death. He lovingly cared for his mom as best he could between his work hours. Fortunately his work assignment had recently shifted from month-long road trips to daytime weekly hours.

God's Nurse

When Carol's health began to decline in May, she re-entered the hospital. I wanted to see her one more time, but I hesitated to intrude on the time with her children who lived in town.

Gathering courage I dialed her hospital room. "Hi Carol.

Wanted to say hello and ask how you are today."

"Pretty weak."

"I was thinking of visiting you—," I began.

"You'd better visit me," she interrupted.

"I could come up on Saturday."

"I'll look forward to seeing you."

I headed north again, stopping briefly at Greig's house to pick up Buster. We headed to Beaufort Memorial, passing old trees that had been there for years. Pulling into the parking lot, I sighed with relief to see a small hospital in a country setting. I welcomed the change from the towering, impersonal one in Savannah and the sprawling complex near the Charleston bay.

Not knowing what to expect I followed Buster into his mom's room.

"Hi, Gail."

Without hesitation I sat on Carol's bed and drew her thin body into a gentle hug. Still holding her hand, I said, "Sure didn't expect to see you here."

"Me either."

Gradually I brought God into our conversation, reminding her that He would hear her prayer. She listened, but didn't appear open to making any decision, though she knew the end was near.

"I know I'm dying, but I want to finish this round of chemo."

She smiled and interacted with ease. My heart wanted to pretend she had a temporary illness and would soon be well. Yet her frail body forced me into reality.

The next day I went by myself. As I knocked and entered her room a nurse stood by Carol's bed.

"She had a rough night," she explained.

"Gail, this is Dot. She's been on call all night. I was so sick."

Carol and I attempted to explain to Dot how we knew each other.

"Well, we used to be sisters-in-law," Carol began.

"After Carol and my brother divorced, we didn't see each other," I continued. "Once Greig got sick, Carol and I became friends again."

"Greig died, but it's like Gail and I are sisters-in-law again."

Dot left and Carol and I talked a few more minutes. Knowing she needed rest, I hugged her and assured her I'd return on Monday.

As I walked into the hallway, Dot came out of an office. We talked about Carol's condition. In the course of our conversation I discovered Dot and I were Christian sisters. After relating some of Carol's background and also my experience of sharing spiritual things with her, I told Dot that she hadn't made any decision for Christ.

Dot smiled. "I'll talk with her this afternoon. I don't have much time to be with patients so I get right to the point. I'll ask if she's ever asked Jesus to be her Lord and Savior. I'll let you know what happens."

I promised to pray for her conversation with Carol and gave her my phone number.

Sister Bond

Dot called me later in the day. "Carol showed reluctance at first, but then she expressed willingness to pray with me. Thank you very much for giving me a chance to take part in this."

"God sent you to us just at the right time," I said.

I explained my plan to visit Carol before leaving town on Monday and told her I'd ask about her experience.

"Please call me after you talk with her," she asked. "Oh, I told her it would be helpful for her to have a Bible and maybe you had one."

The next morning I sat again at Carol's bedside. Pondering how to create an opportunity for her to tell me about her conversation with Dot, I pulled out the small blue Bible I'd brought with me.

"Oh, I need that," she said. "Dot talked to me yesterday and I prayed with her. Then she told me I'm saved!"

I asked, "That's wonderful. What did you experience after you prayed?"

"Peace and release." she replied softly. "Could you read some verses to me?"

I turned to John 3:16, John 14:6 and other verses that confirmed that Jesus had entered her heart when she asked him to and had given her the promise of eternal life with God.

We talked about how Greig would greet her in heaven. While smiling and holding my hand, she gazed at me.

"I don't know why I waited so long. I kept saying, 'No, thank you…no, thank you.'"

"Until yesterday," I replied.

"It helps knowing Greig is there." She paused. "Could you tell Greig's Christian friend? He'll be glad to know I finally made that decision."

I leaned closer. "You know, no matter how many days, weeks or months you have left, God will take you to heaven now that you have accepted His gift of Jesus. He is in your heart because you asked Him to come in."

Carol beamed.

"Now I don't have to say a final goodbye," I said. "I can say, 'Goodbye for now. See you in heaven.'"

My comment brought a shy smile to her face.

"I love you, Carol."

"I love you, too, Gail. Thank you so much for coming."

Reluctantly I hugged her and left her bedside.

Pausing at the door, I turned and waved. "See you in heaven."

Smiling, she waved and replied, "See you in heaven."

Walking down the corridor, my heart exploded with joy. I headed to my dinner with Alisa, who'd become not only our lawyer but my personal friend and God's gift to me. I could hardly wait to tell her about the miracle I'd witnessed. The realization that Carol had a secure place in heaven and I would see her again became a soft shawl draped over my sadness.

When I called Dot later, she was thrilled to hear about Carol's excitement and personal assurance that she would be in heaven. I told her, "I will never forget you. You're doing God's mission. Because of you, Carol accepted God's offer and now she will live in heaven forever."

Carol and I had become true sisters. She resisted until the end. Then in one moment, like a new shoot bursting forth from the dark sod, the miracle of eternal life bloomed in Carol's heart.

God's Timetable

God had arranged for Carol's hospital stay for that particular weekend. I could come during those days. Dot worked only that weekend before being off for a month. As Christian sisters, Dot and I formed God's team to lead Carol to Himself. The private, quiet window of time in the hospital gave Carol a chance to respond to God.

Carol was released the day I left. Once again Buster took his mother to his dad's home. She wanted to finish the full round of chemo before considering hospice but the severe side effects from the next treatment made that impossible. Although a difficult decision, Carol decided to go into hospice, believing she would feel better once she didn't have to struggle with chemo. We felt relief that hospice nurses would come to the house each day.

God also arranged for a personal nurse for Carol—her daughter-in-law Kim. Kim and Jake had flown from Montana with their eight-year-old daughter Bella to visit Carol. When Jake needed to return to work, Bella and Kim, a registered nurse, stayed behind.

God obviously chose Kim as Carol's caregiver for that season of her life.

Kim told me, "I set up a baby monitor in Carol's room. That way if she gets up in the night or moans I'll hear her."

Bella sat in Carol's room often, getting better acquainted with her grandmother. Harley, the beloved family dog, became Bella's companion as well as Carol's bedside guard.

Kim cleaned up the front deck and purchased orange floral cushions. Whenever she felt strong enough, Carol sat outside on the lounge chair drinking in the warmth of the sunshine. Surely during those times she sensed the presence of her newfound God, who was preparing her to live in heaven with Him.

During one hospital visit with Carol, she told me of her desire to still be alive on the first-year anniversary of Greig's death for the sake of her sons.

Carol expressed her wish to Kim. "I'd like the family to have dinner together out on the porch on June 21 in memory of Greig."

That dinner never happened. Too weak to get out of bed, she lay there while Buster, Casey, Kim, and Bella took turns holding her hand and talking with her. Throughout the evening Kim frequently called me with updates.

A mother to the end, Carol willed herself to live through the 21st. One hour after midnight, she took a few peaceful breaths and entered her heavenly home.

I cried when Kim told me. But they were mostly tears of joy. Carol had claimed God as her Savior such a short time before her death, but her decision sealed her eternal home. Now she was together with Greig.

Later Buster told me, "Mom asked me to put some of dad's ashes with hers."

Her request created a sweet picture for me. Carol and Greig had completed their full circle of love.

A Time of Remembrance

Jake, Casey, and Buster had lost both their mother and father within a year. None of us dreamed Greig would die so young. None of us imagined Carol would die so soon after Greig. We all were still stunned by the devastating turn of events.

Carol's brother and sister, David and Leigh, organized a family memorial service in Colorado for Carol and also their mother who had died a month before.

When I picked Buster up on his return from Colorado, he began telling me about his mother's service.

"The service was for my grandmother as well as my mom," he explained. "The pastor talked about Lazarus. He explained how he had died and been buried in the tomb, as my grandmother and mom had been. Then Jesus called to him and he was resurrected. The pastor said my mom and grandmother were buried but they were resurrected."

Buster was uncertain whether God existed and didn't consider Him relevant for his life. In light of his perspective, I was fascinated with the way he had articulated the pastor's message. His explanation provided a longed-for opportunity to tell him the story of his mother's experience with Jesus.

I ended with, "Your mother said, 'I don't know why I waited so long. I kept saying, no, thank you, no, thank you.' I watched your mother go from wondering where she was going when she died to having peace and assurance in her heart that she would be in heaven. She knew she would see your dad there."

Hopeful, I paused.

He responded, "I'm glad for her. I don't believe that way."

"Even though your mother had peace when she died?" I asked.

"I have to have more evidence than that."

Seeds have been planted in Buster's heart, and they are being watered. God is in charge of the harvest and I believe, by faith, that day will come for my nephew.

Another Sister

Buster continued with an amazing story.

"I saw my sister, Kathy," Buster said.

"Your sister?" I asked.

"Yeah, my mother gave her up for adoption. Kathy and her mother flew to Colorado for my mom's service. After Mom had discovered where Kathy lived, she took Casey and me to meet her. Jake met her for the first time this weekend. Before Kathy left she said, 'Why don't we take a family vacation together some time?'"

I smiled at his obvious joy. Kathy's warm suggestion

expanded the boys' sense of family. That invitation couldn't have come at a more important time in their lives.

Months before, while sorting through boxes of pictures at Greig's house, I remembered seeing a picture of Carol with two women and wondered who they were. When Buster and I returned home he confirmed the picture I'd found was taken on the day Carol first met Kathy and her adoptive mother.

Later Regan told me more of the story. When Regan surfaced in Greig's life, and Carol observed the happy ending to their story, she thought about the baby girl she'd given up for adoption when she was only seventeen.

"Greig, I'm thinking about telling the boys about the other sister they don't know they have."

Carol and Kathy's relationship didn't develop into a close one like Greig and Regan's. Still, Carol remained grateful she had found her daughter after all those years.

That timely reunion had given Kathy a chance to celebrate her biological mother's life. Another completed circle. And further evidence of the way God connects the dots in our lives to bring about His plans formed long ago in perfect faithfulness.[9]

PART 2

CONNECTING THE DOTS

WHAT'S THE POINT?

The avalanche of illnesses and deaths in my family ripped through my heart. I felt alone.

Losing Greig wounded me the most. He was my brother, my childhood pal, my peer, my friend. His voice was the one I most longed to hear again. After traveling different roads since our teen years, we had finally joined each other on the same path. When he found Christ at the age of sixty, we became true brother and sister. We both belonged to God's family.

Bombarded with memories of Greig, my tears flowed fiercely and frequently. I couldn't get a grip on life. Grief overpowered my days.

I miss Greig so much. Did he know how much I loved him? Why didn't I say I love you more often? I'd had plenty of opportunities to verbally express my love during his first hospital stay until his last days. But had I?

Surely I could have created more freedom for him to reveal his fears, his feelings of powerlessness, his pain. Why didn't I talk more often about God and read more Scripture to him as spiritual reinforcement for his painful journey? I felt like I'd failed him.

Thoughts of my own mortality also attacked me like diver planes. I talked to God. "What's the point? I try to eat right, exercise, sleep well, and stay healthy. Greig did too, and look what happened to him. I'll become sick one day and die, too. I want to give up. There's no reason to try anymore. Besides, I'll be in heaven with my brother and You."

Darkness. Despair. Regret. Hopelessness. I suffered alone.

On the fourth day of darkness, an unexpected email arrived from Zorina, a long-time friend from the Philippines. Members of the same church, I'd frequently spoken at her youth group. The bond between us led to many personal times together, including family gatherings at her home.

Zorina married her college sweetheart after graduation. When I returned to the States we made no plans to stay in touch. Email wasn't a common convenience then and she'd become a busy mother.

The years blitzed by. Zorina and I hadn't communicated for thirteen years. Until that day.

Hi Gail,

This is Zorn. I've wanted to email you…but with so much work I keep forgetting. I have the chance now since I'm on break from classes. I'm teaching Bible at Small World Christian School. The Lord expanded my territories and is using me for the expansion of His Kingdom. I'm privileged to be used by Him for His glory and I'm enjoying every bit of it.

You know, you've been a part of who I am now. Your mentoring and your encouragement have made me see the light and know God in a very intimate way. I am now the Christian Education Chairperson, Stewardship Chairperson, Praise and Worship leader and the Adult Sunday School teacher. It's overwhelming but I feel blessed.

I've missed you, Gail. When my mom passed away, I asked some church members if they knew your address. I wanted to let you know her going home to the Lord since she was your friend.

I have two beautiful girls…and they want to get to know the Lord more….

I've been blessed by the Lord and couldn't contain my joy and that's why I want to share this to you. I'd like to thank God for you, Gail, for the beautiful moments you've shared with me. I couldn't forget you because you have always been a part of my wonderful life.

God bless you,

Zorn

My hand flew to my mouth as I stared at the screen, captivated by what I'd read. Zorn's words pierced my darkness, allowing God's light to seep in and help me begin to see things from His perspective.

I see, God. I get it. Your Mission. You want me to stay well and healthy so I can continue Your mission on earth. Thank you for reminding me of Your purpose for my existence. You have given me courage and strength to move forward through this unbearable pain.

I called my friend. "Susan, you won't believe what happened." I revealed how God had dramatically illuminated my darkness.

On Friday night I sat with Desi at a nearby ballroom dance studio. When we'd first become acquainted during the weekly dances, he was searching for answers to life. I listened to his questions and encouraged him. Eventually through the influence of many of us in the dance community, Desi embraced God as his own Savior. His faith and his love for God's Word deepened. During twirls around the dance floor, he'd often relate his newest discovery from the Bible.

That particular night he leaned across the table toward me with a scowl on his face. He asked, "Do you ever struggle?"

"Let me tell you about my recent struggle," I began.

After describing my darkness and deep turmoil about my brother's death, I told him about receiving Zorn's email.

"You mean you hadn't heard from her in thirteen years?"

"Right."

"That's amazing." The look of despair lifted and a big smile stretched across his face.

After Desi left our table to dance with his next partner, I shifted to the table where my friend Mary sat.

"I have to tell you about the conversation I had with Desi." Mary learned about the amazing way God had met me in my own time of need and how He had used my experience to remind Desi that God cares about him. Double impact.

Whenever I spotted Desi on the dance floor the rest of the evening, I saw his happy countenance. My heart leaped with joy at this confirmation from God that He still had a mission for me as His ambassador on earth.

Personal Advocates

Greig's death had plunged me into the legal world. I never would have accepted the challenge of handling his estate if his four children had not expressed a desire for their dad's personal representative to be someone other than an heir.

Doubtful and uncertain, I stepped forward. God began pouring out promised provisions. Through the help of Greig's friend Glenn, I located a trusted law firm. The firm assigned me to pretty, twenty-nine-year-old Alisa.

Captured by the unique blend of her legal competence and her warm personality, I joined forces with her. She appreciated my organizational skills while I relished her wise counsel for each step I needed to take.

Many emails flew back and forth. In between my questions about Greig and the property, I often rattled on about the challenges of dealing with the various personalities of my nephews.

One day I commented to Alisa, "I'm sorry I keep telling you about the goings on of my family."

"Don't worry," she said. "Knowing what is happening with the family helps me give you better advice."

As I continued to observe Alisa's compassion for my family, I wondered if she might be a Christian. When I asked if she had a personal relationship with God, she confirmed she did. God had lovingly handpicked Alisa as my lawyer. She stood by my side, not only as my lawyer, but as my friend, my advocate, and my sister in Christ.

Another responsibility loomed—the clearing out of Greig's property. This project encompassed much more than the typical house and small attached garage. His estate included several acres of property, an old house he'd fixed up twelve years before, an expansive detached garage he'd designed and built, a storage shed, and all the machinery and tools he used as a builder. His company tool truck, with organized shelves of tools acquired over a forty-year career, sat in the yard near his work truck and backhoe. The huge garage housed his welding equipment, newer building tools, his extensive array of outdoor sports equipment, his Harley Davidson motorcycle, and many other stored items. His large boat sat near the garage.

My options of either an auction or an estate sale both entailed finding an appraiser to go through all the items and prepare an inventory. I sought the advice of Alisa, who suggested someone who had helped her with two other estates.

Howard agreed to appraise every item on the property and prepare an inventory. However, he also planned to contact every connection he had made over the years—estate buyers, antique dealers, purchasers of scrap metal, personal friends, Habitat for Humanity, and other charitable organizations. He set appointments with those people first, then informed neighbors of the date of an estate sale. Afterwards, he arranged the pickup of the remaining things. Howard's wife, Faith, supervised the crew that did the initial round of cleanup in the house and then personally completed the final cleaning.

Alisa revealed the personal care and attention Howard had given to Buster and Casey. While guiding them in clearing out the things they wanted from their dad's property, he listened to their questions, their reflections about their dad, and their frustrations.

Howard and Faith considered their job finished only after they'd cleared everything from the property so the house could be shown to potential buyers. God knew no one in the family had the time or know-how to accomplish this extensive task.

As I observed all that Howard and Faith had accomplished both professionally and personally, I wondered if they might be Christians. Alisa confirmed it. With the initial payment I included a personal letter of thanks that ended with my tribute: "You are God's gift to our family."

Finally the house sold to a couple who had wanted to find an old house to fix up and had already secured a renovation loan. The house and property Greig had purchased and fixed up would now be enjoyed by someone else. I prayed they would love their home as much as Greig had.

God put His people in my path to help me handle all the details involved in the closing of Greig's estate. The process stretched far beyond the time we had envisioned. This agonizing lag of time made sense only when I connected the dots between people and circumstances. God had woven all of these connections into our lives according to His plan. He had used the time between Greig's illness and death and the closing of his estate to work in the hearts of all of us who'd been left behind.

A CHESSBOARD LIFE

While continuing my journey of grief from Greig's death in June, I realized how physically, emotionally and mentally exhausted I'd become from the months of despair, rising hope, and disappointments.

As I prepared to attend Blair's wedding in September, I had received news of Aunt Elia's illness. Though unfinished grief weighed on my heart and my resources were depleted, I flew to be with the family. Three weeks later, Aunt Elia passed away.

Reflecting on my long journey with Greig and my brief two weeks with my aunt, I evaluated the common denominators: obedience and a willing heart. The obvious variable: the length of time. God revealed another significant difference.

My journey with Greig symbolized the partnership of God and Gail. I allowed God to fill me with His Spirit and relied on His wisdom. I plunged forward with His strength to do everything that needed to be done. God and I walked this faith journey together.

However, during the time I spent with Aunt Elia, I had no emotional or physical strength to devote to a partnership. God operated alone, without Gail. I was present in body only, totally reliant on God.

A picture of those two weeks flashed into my mind. I sensed God taking hold of my hand and helping me step onto His chessboard. Then lovingly He moved me from square to square.

From the beginning of each day until nightfall, I sensed His directions. "Go there. Step here. Say this. Do this. Pause and rest. Now visit that person. Today, don't walk straight ahead; I want you to step back to the previous square."

I felt like I stood in the front row of a chess game of life, watching God work in people's lives and say His words through me. Nothing of "Gail" blocked my vision. I had nothing to offer Him. The Master Planner directed everything that transpired during those two weeks.

Unfolding Plans

God had orchestrated my days at the care center with Aunt Elia and given me a chance to walk at my uncle's side and minister to him. He and I built a new kind of friendship, born out of the inevitable loss we would soon experience.

Being in town allowed me the ease of frequent phone calls with my cousins Blair, Cary, and Pamela. They all provided amazing care for Aunt Elia. Since the three of them worked during the day, I offered to chauffeur my uncle to and from the hospital and do errands. My friendship with my out-of-town cousins Mark and Lynn also deepened. We all worked as a team. A new and wonderful feeling of belonging blossomed inside of me.

Also, being in Portland gave me a chance to connect with Pat. We'd been friends for almost fifty years, ever since I transferred to her high school my sophomore year. Our friendship continued and we stood with each other through many ups and downs.

We'd planned a lunch date. Then I received a call from her.

"Hi, Gail, it's Pat. I know we were going to meet today, but Mother fell last night. We're at Kaiser Hospital."

"Oh no. What's the doctor saying?"

"He says she broke her leg and he's putting her in a cast. Right now I'm working with Rose Villa to see if they have room at their rehab ward. I'll be in touch."

The next day I called her. "How's your mother?"

"You won't believe what happened yesterday," she replied. "As mother and I were leaving the hospital I turned to the doctor and joked, 'Thanks for checking my mother over from head to toe.' He paused and said, 'Well, I didn't actually look at her head. Do you want me to?' I said, 'Well why not. We're here.'"

Pat continued, "We stayed while they did an MRI. Later, the doctor called me in. He told me, 'We have found cancer throughout her body.'"

"Oh, Pat. I can't believe it."

"I know. I told you I was trying to find a room at the rehab center. Next thing I knew I was calling to see if they had a bed in their hospice ward. Fortunately, they did."

"What room is she in? I probably won't be able to come over until later this afternoon but I'll find you."

After helping my aunt, I drove to see Pat and her mother. I meandered a bit, unfamiliar with the surroundings. As I rounded the corner I spotted Pat, hustling down the hallway in search of a nurse to administer another pain shot for her mother.

We embraced each other. When she needed me most, I was there.

After requesting the shot, Pat looped her hand through my arm and guided me to her mother's room. Alice moaned with pain, but as I came into view she smiled.

"Hello, Gail. I'm glad to see you. I'm not doing well right now. Could you come by tomorrow?"

Clasping her hand and gazing into her sweet face, I told her, "I hope so."

That was our last conversation. Her mother died three days later.

What If?

What if I had resisted God's prompting to travel to Portland since I felt exhausted? What if I'd not taken God's hand and stepped onto His chessboard?

By saying yes to God's leading, I experienced final healing in my relationship with Aunt Elia. Her parting words to me wiped away all the hurt I'd felt in our relationship. When she put her arms around me and we said goodbye, I knew she loved me.

By saying yes to God, I'd been able to step into Pat's crumbling world and support her when death crept in. I had the sweet privilege of saying goodbye to her mother, who had loved me and treated me as a daughter. Pat also had a chance to encourage me during my own traumatic journey with my aunt's illness.

My choice to step onto God's chessboard and totally depend on His direction throughout those two weeks allowed me to be exactly where He needed me to be each day. God created conversations and connections that encouraged and gave life to my family and friends and breathed life and strength into me as well.

God revealed a powerful message to me during my time of reflection. Live moment by moment, day by day in the power of God's Spirit. I realized I hadn't resisted God's direction or tried to jump ahead of Him throughout those two weeks. Incapable of forming any plan of my own, I simply followed His instructions. I moved from person to person, place to place, situation to situation totally dependent on His strength and ability. Too exhausted to think of words to speak, I simply listened to God and said what He wanted me to say. I longed to live that way always.

Sarah Young, in her book, *Jesus Calling*, imagined Jesus saying to us, "Miracles are not always visible to the naked eye, but those who live by faith can see them clearly. Living by faith, rather than sight, enables you to see My Glory."[10]

I'd had a chance to catch a glimpse of God's glory. Wanting to record a prayer of thanksgiving and recommitment, I opened my journal.

Thank you, God, for holding my hand and helping me step onto your chessboard. Thank you for walking through each day with me. This is the kind of life you desire me to live. I never want to go back to a 'God and Gail partnership.' I want you to be CEO all the time. I want to follow Your call.

Your plan. Your decision. Your schedule. Your Directive. I want to reflect Your heart of compassion to those around me.

Don't ever let me give up my special front-row seat in the Game of Life you are unfolding. Open my eyes to see your work every day. Help me to be consumed by Your purpose for me rather than trying to plan my own life.

Help me live by faith not by sight. Remind me to allow Your Spirit to move me to each square on Your chessboard where you want me to be throughout the day. Show me the role you want me to play in each situation and prompt me to speak Your words. Help me live out the plan You ordained for me before the foundation of the world.

NEXT STEPS

"Jake and I plan to go on a cycle run together in North Carolina the week of June 21."

I smiled as I learned about Buster's plan to spend time with his older brother. Two years had passed since they'd lost their father and one year after saying goodbye to their mother. What a perfect plan for two cyclists who love roaming through beautiful scenery.

After their trip I said, "So glad you and Jake could go. Did you talk about your mom and dad while you were together?"

"We didn't talk about them. We both knew we were together and it was good. Want to see a video I took from my cycle?"

"Sure," I said, jotting down the title to search for on his Facebook page.

When I watched the video, I felt the wind blowing through my hair as I rode with him through the winding roads of the Blue Ridge Mountains on that bright, sunny day. Catching a glimpse of their exhilaration connected me to their world.

Recently, Buster called me to say his car had been stolen the night before from the house of a friend. I felt sorry that he suddenly had no transportation and faced the trouble of finding another car.

As I pondered his situation, my heart sank even lower. That car belonged to his dad and was part of Buster's inheritance.

When I called Buster that night to get an update on his car

hunting, I told him I prayed God would return his car. His lack of response didn't surprise me. I knew he didn't feel any need to make God a part of this event.

The next morning I received a text. *Friend found my car last night around midnight. Went and got it. Nothing missing and seems to be no damage to it.*

I texted back. *Wow…that's amazing! So glad for you. Thanks for letting me know. Guess God heard my prayer?! Seemed an impossible request at the time but He makes things possible.* ☺

Best Friends

Casey left me a voicemail one day. "Aunt Gail, I called to tell you an *amazing* story I know you will want to hear. Text me a good time to call you."

Finally catching up with each other, he related his story. "Eric, my best friend for fifteen years here, now lives in Tennessee. We call each other twin—I mean, we look alike, talk alike, we have the same gestures. Everyone gets us mixed up.

"Anyway, on December 23 I felt a strong urge to call him. I had to leave a voicemail but I ended with, 'Miss you twin. I love you.'

"On December 24 I noticed him on Facebook and left him a message. 'Hey, I guess your phone is broken?' He responded, 'Bro, I saw your message but was waiting for more than five minutes so we could talk. Miss you. Love you to death.'

"Christmas morning I got a message from a friend. At 1 a.m. Eric's car spun out on black ice and he died."

"Oh, Casey, I'm so sorry. Can't imagine how you feel."

"I couldn't believe it. I really wanted to go to the service but it was in Tennessee. The following Friday night I was lying on my bed thinking about Eric. I felt the strongest urge to drive up to Tennessee. I didn't know anyone there but I had to go."

Once he arrived he remembered a place Eric liked to hang out with friends. Walking in the door, he heard gasps and cries from many of Eric's friends.

One gal rushed over to Casey and said, "You look just like Eric. But he's gone. What are we supposed to do now?"

Casey answered, "I believe Eric would want us to celebrate his life."

That led to a time of storytelling as Eric's friends gathered around Casey. Pretty soon they were laughing instead of crying. Casey's presence gave them the gift of feeling like they had been with Eric one more time.

Someone gave him the phone number of Eric's mother, so he connected with her the next day. His likeness to her son soothed this mother's heart and bridged her emptiness for those moments.

By the time Casey returned home and logged on to Facebook, messages from many of his new friends flooded his screen. He read them to me over the phone and later emailed some of the messages.

Thank u for being u and reminding everyone to remember Eric. U r amazing.

Eric's lovely twin that I'm so glad I had a chance to meet! Thank you so much for coming up to spread the love and happiness for him.

You are one of the most amazing people I've met in a long time. Thank you for your visit. You have a wonderful spirit! You were such a blessing and can't wait to see you again.

He responded, *You know, I've had a LOT of bad things happen to me over the past few years, but I'd rather they happen to me than any one of you. I love you all. Happy New Year!*

As he finished telling me his story, I asked about Eric. He then read me a message Eric had posted earlier in the year. *What an incredible day. At the end of my rope God throws me a blessing that reminds me why we go through trials in life. If you are going through trials no matter how big or small keep your faith. God has something incredible in store for you. Without going into detail, God floored me today.*

We both felt confident Eric lived in heaven. But faced with the sudden death of his friend, Casey expressed doubt he would go to heaven, too. He'd accepted Christ with me at an early age. After I re-entered his life as a result of Greig's illness, we'd had various opportunities to talk about Jesus and he'd asked for a Bible. I reminded him of our conversations and asked him, "You said you have accepted Jesus. Is He in your heart?"

"Yes," he confirmed.

"Then you will be in heaven." I assured him. "And, Casey, those urgings you felt were from God. You responded and said yes. You called Eric in time and you went to Tennessee where God used you to encourage Eric's friends. You've had a taste of what it's like to let God lead your life. So you don't need to have one more moment

151

of doubt that God is in your life."

He got it. We had talked many times about the importance of letting Christ be not only his Savior but also His Lord. Now he had a visual picture, his own personal experience, and finally it made sense to him.

From then on, we continued to talk about God and God's desire for his life. Casey shifted away from responding as a victim and slowly began to live more often as a victor by allowing God to direct his life. Through many ups and downs in life, I've seen him calm down, turn away from his usual anger, and embrace a more positive line of thinking. Casey has begun to know God as a real person who loves him and cares about his daily life.

An example surfaced recently. Desperate to leave his unpleasant housing situation with two roommates, he vented his frustrations. He was especially concerned about their behavior because his daughter Piper stayed with him every other weekend.

The next weekend he sent me two texts, each expressing high stress. The third one said, *Picked up Piper for the weekend. We're going to look for places.*

I texted back, *I will ask God to lead the two of you to a place that will be peaceful for you.*

I laughed at his response. *Let me know what he says, try to get the address! LOL*

LOL, you're cute. Fortunately u r familiar with his 'nudges' so stay tuned in!

Subsequent text messages and phone calls reflected the new

relationship we share. I'm grateful I am in his life, not only as his aunt but as his friend. Like all of us, he'll have setbacks. Yet, if he continues to choose God's way, he will have the power to live a different kind of life.

None of my previous conversations with him had led to any lasting change. His personal desire to change didn't make a difference either. Only his devastation over the loss of his best friend opened his heart to hear God, follow His leading, and experience a new kind of life. I'm standing by to see what God does next in his life.

Montana Connection

My oldest nephew Jake lives in Montana. I'd not seen him for more than twenty years at the time of Greig's death. Jake was a teenager when Greig had brought him and Casey to Mom's memorial service. Sightseeing and family gatherings during those days gave me a glimpse into Jake's serious personality.

Past memories of him faded as I hugged his tall, trim frame when he arrived in South Carolina. His deep voice, contagious laughter, and charming smile captured my heart.

Although the next days were filled with agonizing family decisions, I relished the chance to get to know him better. The day I hugged Jake goodbye I felt like crying. I had no idea when I would see him again.

"Let's stay in touch," I said.

"Definitely," he responded with a smile.

Recently I expressed my desire to talk with his eight-year-old daughter Bella.

"She's coming during the Christmas holiday. Why don't we try to connect then?"

Jake made it happen. Bella and I talked after one of their days of skiing. We talked like it was a common occurrence, though she and I had not met each other yet.

Another call with Jake further strengthened our relationship even more. We talked about his work life, his daughter, and memories of his growing up years.

"It's been nice talking with you," he said as we finished our conversation. Our exchange of "I love you" that day rang more true than ever before. I believe he realized how much I love him and care about what happens in his life.

"Remember to send me pictures of Bella when you can."

The next morning four adorable pictures landed in my in-box. I'm catching up on Jake's life, and loving being a true aunt to him.

Great, Great Aunt

I used to see Regan occasionally while visiting my aunt and the family during my furloughs from the Philippines. Though I thoroughly enjoyed our conversations when we were together, I didn't necessarily make a point to see her. She was my niece, but I hadn't taken steps to become part of her life.

Now, because of our shared journey of Greig's illness and the chance to be together during his last days of life, we have a close relationship. I will never again pass up an opportunity to be with her and her family.

As if to accentuate our new relationship, God brought someone else into our lives—Regan's granddaughter Ariella. I had followed the pregnancy of my great niece Anjela. Finally the day arrived. A text beeped on my phone. *Anjela had her baby last night* ☺ *Ariella 6 lb 9 oz.*

We continued texting back and forth. Near the end of our dialogue I read one surprising text. *Hey u r a great-great aunt* ☺ *I love and miss you lots xoxo.*

Shocked into reality, I texted back, *You r right!! I must be very old! LOL Miss you esp at times like this xoxo.*

Two months later, during my yearly visit, Regan and I sat together in her living room. I couldn't stop gazing into the beautiful face of little Ariella as she rested in my arms.

Regan said, "Aunt Gail, you said you felt old as a great-great aunt. So I got to thinking. We can call you G-G Gail!" We laughed. Her concern about my personal feelings touched me.

As Easter approached a card arrived. Inside she'd written, "To my Dearest Aunt." The sentiment of the card brought tears to my eyes.

> *You have a wonderful way of making people feel so special…*
> *so loved. The kind and thoughtful things you do bring*
> *special warmth to our family. Thank you for being the*
> *kind of aunt who always takes the time to care.*

Redemption from Death

While Greig was ill, unknowingly he beckoned me to take a new road, a road that would help set me free from my fear of rejection. He led me into the lives of his children and gave me the opportunity to be a participant in his family.

He walked beside me and listened, advised, and encouraged me in this unfamiliar territory. With little time to focus on my fear, I grew stronger emotionally. Slowly I gained courage to live in a more open way and express genuine love to the family.

When Greig died, a part of my heart died. But his death redeemed me. Greig left me with the gift of his four children who would keep me involved in life.

The new relationships I share with these four dear people have replaced my loneliness with fulfillment. I have many opportunities to listen, to encourage, to cry with them in their sad times, and to rejoice with them in their victories. Challenges sprout up. Disappointments surface in their lives and mine. But all these things have led to greater understanding between us.

"I tell you the truth, unless a kernel of wheat is planted in the soil and dies, it remains alone. But its death will produce many new kernels—a plentiful harvest of new lives,"[11]

Greig's death is beginning to produce a harvest. God's work started with me, and it's spreading to his children.

Roadway in the Wilderness

God said in Isaiah 43:18-19. "Do not call to mind the former things, or ponder things of the past. Behold, I will do something new, now it will spring forth; will you not be aware of it? I will even make a roadway in the wilderness, rivers in the desert."

I wasn't aware of my wandering. I didn't realize that my choice to stay isolated from my family had created loneliness in my heart. God used the illnesses and deaths in my family to break down the walls and bridge the distance. With my heart exposed, I faced a choice: to step back into my old familiar life as a spectator or step forward as a participant in the lives of those who were left behind. I chose to trust God and step forward.

Tears continue to flow at times as I remember Greig and the others who now live in heaven. But because of my losses, I'm walking on God's roadway of freedom and drinking from His river.

For me, it took the broken heart of loss to find true life.

CONCLUSION

Where are you on your journey of loss? You will have to pass through a cycle of grief. You have no choice. But the journey is not without hope, because God will be by your side.

During my first loss, a friend gave me a diagram called "A Grief Cycle for God's People." The cycle included five possible stages from loss to healing.

1. <u>Initial Impact</u>: Shock, numbness, denial, hopelessness
2. <u>Wrestling with the pain</u>: Emotional distress, emotional expression, physical symptoms, guilt, loneliness, isolation
3. <u>Wrestling with reality</u>: Longing for what was lost, distorted perception, depression
4. <u>Turning or returning to God</u>: Alienation from God, wavering, confession of sin, reaching out to God, remembering God's love, claiming God's promises
5. <u>Moving toward healing</u>: Waiting on God, choosing to rejoice, new relationships, new hope, acceptance, helping others[12]

Identifying with some of these stages helped me realize my responses were normal and others traveled on the same journey with me.

The psalmist David begins many of his songs in desperation, crying out to the Lord for help. By the end of the psalm he has found his hope, his strength, and his salvation in God.

158

You know my stories. I've painted my pain for you. You've watched my heart break. You've seen God reveal His work in my life and give me hope in the midst of my pain.

If only you could share your story with me, I could begin to understand your pain. Yet, I would never be able to feel it the way God does. He sees each tear that escapes from your eye and runs down your cheek.

King David said to God, "You have taken account of my wanderings; put my tears in Your bottle. Are *they* not in Your book?"[13]

Not one tear evaporates. He captures all of your tears in His bottle—preserves them—because they represent pain that you, His precious child, have endured.

Paul reminds us, "For momentary, light affliction is producing for us an eternal weight of glory far beyond all comparison, while we look not at the things which are seen, but at the things which are not seen; for the things which are seen are temporal, but the things which are not seen are eternal."[14]

At times you may feel as though you will die from the heartbreak of losing someone you love. Your soul seems dark; your spirit dry.

God is aware of the sorrow and pain that rip through your soul and He understands. He said goodbye to His one and only Son, feeling in that moment as though His broken heart would never heal. But He planned the day of resurrection.

Resurrection is the culmination of your hope that you will see daylight again. God promises to turn your mourning into joy. He will comfort you and give you joy for your sorrow. He promises to give you a garland instead of ashes, the oil of gladness instead of mourning, the mantle of praise instead of a spirit of fainting.[15] David says, "Weeping may last for the night, but a shout of joy comes in the morning."[16]

Resurrection morning may dawn in your heart tomorrow, days from now, or months from now. Grieving takes time and you must travel that road. But don't lose hope. You can begin to experience release, relief, and joy the moment you realize you don't need to live forever with your sorrow. As you lift your eyes and focus on Him, you will realize He is your deliverer from sorrow, your hope for tomorrow.

Your part is to surrender. Sarah Young expressed God's perspective of letting go in *Jesus Calling*.

"This is a time in your life when you must learn to let go: of loved ones, of possessions, of control. In order to let go of something that is precious to you, you need to rest in My presence, where you are complete. Take time to bask in the light of My love. As you relax more and more, your grasping hand gradually opens up, releasing your prized possession into My care."[17]

As you let go of your sorrow and lift your eyes to the One who cares so much for you, you will be able to discover the life that awaits you on the other side of your grief. Out of the brokenness of your heart, God will create a new life, a different life for you. As you step forward, you will see the picture more clearly.

Reaching for New Life

Moving toward a new life is scary. You may be afraid if you let go of your sorrow you will forget the person.

Christine Cleary lost her husband to cancer when he was 44. She says, "Death forces you to look back, and acceptance involves slowly turning your body around to look forward. If you begin a new chapter of life, you carry the person you lost along with you."

"Anyone who has lost a loved one knows that you don't 'recover'. Instead, you learn to incorporate their absence and memories into your life and channel your emotional energy toward others. Eventually, it has been said, your grief walks beside you instead of consuming you."[18]

A widower told me, "The sharp pain from the death of my wife has now changed to a dull ache."

Holly Prigerson, Director of the Center for Psycho-oncology and Palliative Care Research at Dana-Farber Cancer Institute, explains, "In general, bereaved survivors shouldn't think of 'getting over' a loss, but develop ways to get used to it. Even years after someone dies, pangs of grief may come out of the blue, and feelings of heartache and missing the deceased are rekindled. That's normal."

Evelyn Husband-Thompson lost her husband Rick, commander of the space shuttle *Colombia*. After a seventeen-day science mission, *Colombia* headed toward earth but disintegrated upon re-entering the atmosphere on February 1, 2003. That day Evelyn stepped onto a "very difficult road" with "lots of tears and lots of pain."

Though remarried she said, "We have gone through a difficult journey of loss…and we're still on that road."

She has found comfort in her faith and through volunteering with Fathers in the Field, an organization seeking to help fatherless boys. She would have "given anything" to have found this kind of program while raising her seven-year-old son and twelve-year-old daughter alone.

Other surviving spouses of the *Colombia* disaster changed courses after the tragedy. Dr. Jonathan Clark, widower to Laurel Clark, committed himself to the crusade of astronaut safety. Rona Ramon, widow of Israeli astronaut Ilan Ramon, became a grief counselor after dealing with the loss of her husband and also of their son, a budding fighter pilot killed in a training accident.[19]

More recently a girlfriend and boyfriend, Laura and Eddie, from the same high school lost their lives in a car accident due to not wearing seat belts. When her son Eddie died, Lorisse wasn't sure how to carry on. "Tragedies, however, sometimes take survivors down unexpected paths," she said.

Lorisse and the mother of Laura were determined to carry on with purpose, mostly because of their other children. They had heard that often parents who lose children become so absorbed in their grief that their surviving children feel like they have lost their parents. So both mothers and the entire school community began a crusade. The students organized a blood drive at school to celebrate the lives of classmates who survived the wreck. They began spreading the word about the importance of wearing seat belts. Then someone developed a sticker and logo. Next a new cause was born: ALWAYS WEAR YOUR SEATBELT for Laura Grant and Eddie Culberhouse.

This cause has given the families and friends of these two young people a continuing opportunity to help insure that no one—especially teen-agers—lose their life due to a failure to click on their seat belt. These people are making a difference.[20]

People left behind need a reason to go on living. That truth was vividly experienced and documented by Victor Frankl, a prominent Jewish psychiatrist and neurologist in Vienna who became a Nazi survivor.

In September 1942, he was arrested and transported to a Nazi concentration camp with his wife and parents. Three years later, when his camp was liberated, most of his family, including his pregnant wife, had perished—but he lived.

In 1946 he wrote a book, *Man's Search for Meaning*. He concluded that the difference between those who had lived and those who had died rested on only one thing: meaning. Those who found meaning, even in those terrifying circumstances, were able to withstand deplorable suffering; those without meaning did not.

"Everything can be taken from a man but one thing, the last of the human freedoms—to choose one's attitude in any given set of circumstances...." he stated in his book.

He cites the example of two suicidal inmates who chose to live. These men were hopeless and believed there was nothing more to expect from life, nothing to live for. As a therapist in the camps,

Frankl helped them realize that life was "still expecting something from them; something in the future was expected of them." One man chose to live because of his young child who was then living in a foreign country. The other one, a scientist, became determined to finish a series of books he had started."[21]

The story of Ruth in the Bible also highlights the result of choices and perspective. Both Naomi and Ruth experienced the traumatic loss of their husbands, with Naomi also losing her two sons. Both of these women had a choice to make.

Interestingly, Israelite Naomi returned to her homeland with a negative view of herself and her life. She told her women friends, "...Do not call me Naomi; call me Mara, because the Almighty has made my life very bitter. I went away full, but the Lord has brought me back empty. Why call me Naomi? The LORD has afflicted me; the Almighty has brought misfortune upon me."[22]

In contrast, Ruth, from the pagan land of Moab, had a positive view of things. She told Naomi, "...Your people will be my people and your God, my God."[23] In the midst of her sadness and loss, Ruth looked to her new God and made a choice to leave her home and accompany Naomi as her comforter.

We can become victims of our perception of our circumstances. Naomi felt she was returning empty. In God's eyes, Naomi returned with a trophy of God's grace—Ruth—the woman who would become part of the Messianic line.

In a time of need, God led Ruth to Boaz, who would become her kinsman-redeemer—a symbol of Christ, our Redeemer. He told her, "Now, my daughter, do not fear. I will do for you whatever you ask, for all my people in the city know that you are a woman of excellence...I will redeem you."[24]

God enabled Ruth to bear a son, who filled Naomi's heart with fullness and happiness again. Through the line of that child our Redeemer would be born.[25]

What if Ruth had stayed in her homeland, focusing on her loss and trying to make the best of her life? She could have stayed with her familiar life in her home country and remained alone. Instead, she chose to embrace a positive attitude, in spite of her tragic circumstances, and to step forward with courage into the land and life God had prepared for her.

Discovering Your New Purpose

God offers you a new and special life, just as He did for Ruth. He knows your heartache and your circumstances.

You can pour out your heart to Him. Ask Him to ease your pain and show you what next step you could take to discover His purpose for your new season. He doesn't intend for you to figure out your own plan. He wants you to turn things over to Him so He can guide your steps in the way He knows is best for you.

If you have only an ounce of emotional energy left, that's enough to take that first faltering step of faith. God will take your hand, lift your head, and enable you to find His direction for you.

He has placed passions deep inside you. As you begin to recognize them, they will stir your heart. You may notice unique qualities and characteristics you didn't know you had. He gave you those abilities to equip you for what lies ahead.

Your loss may open the way to leave your own unique footprints in the lives of other people. Your immediate family is a good place to start. What remaining family members need you? In what ways were you providing nourishment and encouragement before loss gripped you? Continue that mission. They may need you to listen and be there for them. Perhaps your loss has carved out more time in your days than you had before. Take advantage.

Where could you share your story? Sometimes talking about your experience helps you personally. Explaining your story can also open a door for a friend to say, "I identify with you. That's exactly what I'm feeling. Can you help me?" Purpose can be born in that moment.

What new ways can you become involved in your community, your church, your school? Your involvement might become a way to preserve the memory of your loved one. Or you may uncover something your family can do together. Participating in certain kinds of events might create a way to speak out against injustice or danger, or raise funds to find a cure for the disease that took your loved one's life.

Your outgoing personality might draw you to a speaking platform. If you have a quiet, reserved nature, that quality may lead to many meaningful one-on-one conversations with your neighbors, or hurting people in a chemo ward, rehab center, or crisis counseling center.

New Beginnings

As you travel your new road, ask God to help you identify the ways He is connecting people and circumstances in your life. Think about the conversations you've been able to have because of your loss. Consider new relationships that may have blossomed. Notice the transformation He is making in your life.

If you are still feeling hopeless today, ask God to lift you and carry you forward. If you've already started walking again but are unsure which direction to head, ask Him. He will lead you into things that can make life seem worth living again.

If God is not yet a part of your life, why not open your heart to Him now? Tell Him, through a simple prayer in your own words, that you want to begin a relationship with Him. He desires to become your Redeemer, your Comforter, your Guide, and your Friend.

Loss doesn't need to spell the end of life for you. As Brenda Sprayue expressed, "Although life is full of endings, it's also full of beginnings."[26]

You can begin a moment-by-moment, step-by-step journey with the living God who loves you unconditionally. As you follow Him each day, you can discover and experience His unique purpose for you.

Life may be waiting for you just around the bend. Take that first step forward. God will be waiting for you there.

GAIL PORTER

QUESTIONS FOR THE HEART

Facing Your Pain

1. What kind of loss have you experienced? The loss of a parent? A spouse? A child? A sibling? Close friend? Describe your loss.

2. What was your initial response?

3. What does the verse about God "catching your tears in a bottle" mean to you personally? (Psalm 56:8)

4. What words or actions of others have brought you the most comfort as you've tried to make sense of your loss?

5. In the times you felt emotionally, mentally, physically or spiritually depleted, how did God lead you? In those times did you experience a Chessboard Life (Chapter 9)? Explain your experience.

6. Do you have regrets about your care giving or time spent with the one who was suffering, like I experienced with my brother? What do you do when those kinds of regrets surface? Ponder the relevance of Romans 8:1 and 1 Peter 5:8 for your situation.

Finding Your Purpose

1. In what ways has the promise contained in Philippians 1:6 encouraged you? Explain.

2. What "God connections" have you recognized on your unexpected journey? In what ways has the discovery of those connections softened your sadness?

3. How have some of those connections changed your perspective on life, according to Romans 8:28? Give examples.

4. What is one "next step" you have taken? In what way has that helped you make progress in finding your purpose?

5. Are there areas of service or giving that you want to explore? Explain.

6. In what ways have your priorities in life shifted as a result of your loss? Has God's promise in Isaiah 43:18-19 become true for you? Explain.

7. What ways have you been able to encourage or minister to members of your family?

8. Have you had a chance to comfort someone else because of your experience (2 Corinthians 1:3-4)? Explain.

9. Have you sensed a "second chance" through helping others? How has that impacted your life?

10. If you have begun to experience joy again, what do you think has made the greatest difference in bringing you to that point in your life? Reflect on Isaiah 61:1-3.

NOTES

END NOTES

1 2 Cor. 4:17, 18.

2 2 Cor. 5:1.

3 John 11: 25, 26.

4 Rom. 8:1.

5 Ps. 17:8.

6 Zeph. 3:17.

7 Deut. 33:27.

8 Ps. 91:4.

9 Ps. 25:1.

10 Sarah Young, *Jesus Calling* (Tennessee: Thomas Nelson, Inc., 2008), December 21 reading.

11 John 12:24 (New Living Translation).

12 *A Grief Cycle for God's People* (One-page diagram from an unidentified source).

13 Ps. 56:8.

14 2 Cor. 4:17-18.

15 Jer. 31:13; Isa. 61:3.

16 Ps. 30:5 b (New International Version).

17 Sarah Young, *Jesus Calling*, (Tennessee: Thomas Nelson, Inc., 2008), March 24 reading.

18 Source unknown.

19 Mark K. Matthews, "Commander's widow cherishes final conversation," *Orlando Sentinel*, February 1, 2012, A10.

[20] Scott Maxwell, "Teen couple's tragedy gives birth to new crusade," *Orlando Sentinel*, March 27, 2013, accessed online on March 28, 2013.

[21] Emily Esfahani Smith, "There's More To Life Than Being Happy," *The Atlantic*, January 9, 2013.

[22] Ruth 1:20-21 (New International Version).

[23] Ruth 1:16.

[24] Ruth 3:11, 13 b.

[25] Freedom in Christ Bible, New International Version, (Michigan: Zondervan, 1973, 1978, 1984), Book of Ruth, 288.

[26] Brenda Sprayue. 2003. "Saying Goodbye," *Today's Christian Women*, September-October issue, 80.

36859135R00112

Made in the USA
Lexington, KY
11 November 2014